Cooking for Two

Cover and interior imagery © Debbie G. Harman.

Design copyrighted 2007 by Covenant Communications, Inc.
Published by Covenant Communications, Inc.
American Fork, Utah

Printed in China
First Printing: September 2007

13 12 11 10 09 08 07   10 9 8 7 6 5 4 3 2 1

ISBN 978-1-59811-363-1

MORMON PANTRY

Cooking for Two

Debbie G. Harman

A collection of quick and easy recipes
sized just right for... two.

Table of Contents

Planning Your Meals

- Plan a weekly menu using the advertised sales from your local grocers and using seasonal produce like squash, tomatoes, apples, etc.

- Use variety when planning meals. If you have a tomato-based meal like spaghetti one night, the next night plan a potato or white sauce base.

- Plan meals that will allow you to stay within your budget. Plan soups and casseroles for a few meals, but at least one nice meal each week.

- Plan a well-balanced menu. Make sure you cover the basic food groups. Plan your dinners first and then fill in missing nutrients with breakfast and lunch. Remember the reason we eat is to give our bodies the . . . NUTRIENTS THEY NEED! You will be healthier and happier if you prepare nutritious meals.

♥ Don't Forget Your VITAMINS ♥

VITAMIN-A ♥ For healthy skin and eyes boosts your immune system
SOURCES: sweet potatoes, carrots, squash, apricots, peaches, red peppers, cantaloupe, spinach, broccoli, dairy products, eggs

VITAMIN-B
♥ Regulates appetite and digestion
Healthy nervous system
Sources: Whole Wheat, Meat, Dairy

VITAMIN-C ♥ Strong bones and teeth, repairs cells. Helps to cure the common cold.
SOURCES: Bell Peppers, brussels sprouts, strawberries, oranges, broccoli, parsley, red cabbage, kiwifruit, and cauliflower.

VITAMIN-E ♥ Helps prevent Heart Disease and blood clots
Builds red blood cells
SOURCES: Leafy greens, asparagus, wheat germ, peanuts, almonds, butter, meat, sunflower seeds

Let's Go Shopping

- Make a list from your menu of needed items and take your shopping list with you.

- Stay within your budget. It may take a few months to know how much to budget for food...then stick to it!

- Allow about 20% of your budget to stock up on sale items and in-store specials. You can build storage now.

- When stocking up on sale items, be sure to buy only what you can use. Read expiration dates.

- Shop when you can take your time to compare values and get exactly what you need.

- Don't shop when you are hungry and don't take your husband unless he is a disciplined shopper.

Time to Stock the Pantry

Stock your pantry with items that you will use often. Here is a list of some basic foods that you may want to keep in supply. These items frequently go on sale.

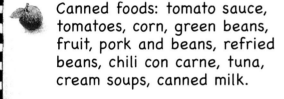 Canned foods: tomato sauce, tomatoes, corn, green beans, fruit, pork and beans, refried beans, chili con carne, tuna, cream soups, canned milk.

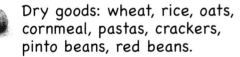 Dry goods: wheat, rice, oats, cornmeal, pastas, crackers, pinto beans, red beans.

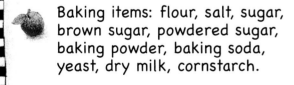 Baking items: flour, salt, sugar, brown sugar, powdered sugar, baking powder, baking soda, yeast, dry milk, cornstarch.

Extra baking items: raisins, nuts, chocolate chips, cocoa, vanilla and other extracts.

Condiments: ketchup, mustard, mayonnaise, vinegar, soy sauce, Worcestershire sauce, pickles, olives, peanut butter, honey.

3

Substitution Guide

1/4 cup **brown sugar**---1/4 cup sugar + 2 Tbsp. maple syrup

1/4 cup **powdered sugar**---1/4 cup sugar (blend to powder in blender)

1 Tbsp. **baking powder**---1 tsp. baking soda + 2 tsp. cornstarch

1 **egg**---3 Tbsp. mayonnaise

1 Tbsp. **butter**---1 Tbsp. margarine

1/4 cup **vegetable oil**---1/2 cube butter or margarine, melted

1/4 cup **buttermilk**---1/4 cup milk + 1 Tbsp. vinegar

1/4 cup **cream**---1/4 cup canned milk

1/4 cup **canned milk**---1/4 cup milk + 1 Tbsp. dry milk

1/4 cup **sour cream**---3 Tbsp. milk + 1 Tbsp. vinegar + 1 Tbsp. butter

1/2 cup **cream of chicken soup**---1/3 cup white sauce + 1/4 cup chicken stock

1/2 cup **cream of celery soup**---1/3 cup white sauce + 1/4 cup chicken stock + 1/4 cup chopped celery

1/2 cup **cream of mushroom** soup---1/3 cup white sauce + 3 Tbsp. chopped mushrooms + 3 Tbsp. beef stock

1/4 cup **walnuts**---1/2 cup rolled oats

1 Tbsp. **red wine vinegar**---1 Tbsp. apple cider vinegar

1 Tbsp. **white wine vinegar**---1 Tbsp. white vinegar

1 Tbsp. **Worcestershire sauce**---2 tsp. soy sauce + 1 tsp. vinegar

Breakfast to Brunch

Breakfast to Brunch

Breakfast is my husband's favorite meal. He can eat pancakes and eggs any time of the day. When we go to bed at night he will ask what we're going to have for breakfast in the morning. I am more of the brunch type. I like to be up and around for a few hours before eating. Whether you like breakfast or brunch, this section is filled with my favorites!

Breads

I have also included many favorite bread recipes in these pages. You'll find them at the end of the section.

Ken's Perfect Pancakes

1 cup all-purpose flour
2 tsp. baking powder
1 Tbsp. sugar
1/2 tsp. salt

1 egg
2 Tbsp. oil
1 cup milk

Mix dry ingredients together. (Ken's secret to perfect pancakes is to fluff the dry ingredients with a wire wisk for a few minutes.) Beat egg, oil, and milk together until well blended. Pour into dry ingredients and stir just until moist. Drop onto hot oiled griddle. Cook until bubbles appear all over and edges are browned. Turn and cook other side. (Do not flip more than once and do not press pancake down.)

Blueberry Pancakes

Follow the above directions and add 1/4 cup fresh or canned blueberries. If you use canned blueberries, be sure to rinse them. (Note: save the juice to make blueberry syrup)

Blueberry Syrup

1/4 cup blueberry juice   1/2 cup sugar   1/2 cup water

Mix sugar and water in saucepan. Bring to a boil and boil 5 minutes without stirring. Turn off heat. Stir in blueberry juice. Cool 5 minutes before serving.

Blender Whole Wheat Pancakes

2 Tbsp. butter
1/2 cup milk
1 egg
1/2 cup whole wheat

1/4 tsp. baking soda
1/2 tsp. salt
2 Tbsp. honey or sugar

Blend wheat on high until a coarse flour is made. Add milk, butter, and egg and continue to blend. Blend in remaining ingredients. Pour 3-4" circles of batter onto a hot greased griddle. Cook until bubbles appear all over and edges start to brown. Turn and cook other side. Serve with maple syrup These pancakes also taste good with chunky peach topping.

Chunky Peach Topping

1 16-oz. can sliced peaches
1/4 cup brown sugar
1 Tbsp. butter
1/4 cup water

Melt butter in saucepan. Stir in sugar, water, peaches, and the peach juice from the can. Mash peaches with potato masher into small chunks. Bring to a boil and boil for 5 minutes, stirring occasionally. Turn off heat and allow to cool a few minutes before serving. Tastes great on whole wheat pancakes.

German Pancakes

2 Tbsp. butter   1/2 cup flour
3 eggs   1/4 tsp. salt
1/2 cup milk

Place butter in 8" x 8" cake pan and put in oven to melt. (Don't let it burn!) Beat eggs. Stir in milk, flour, and salt. Mix well. Pour batter over melted butter. Bake at 450 for 15 to 20 minutes or until edges are golden brown.

Homemade Maple Syrup

1/2 cup sugar   1/2 tsp. maple flavoring
1/2 cup water   2 Tbsp. corn syrup (opt.)

Mix water and sugar (and corn syrup if desired) in a small saucepan. Bring to a boil, stirring until sugar dissolves. Boil 5 minutes without stirring. Remove from heat and stir in maple flavoring.

Homemade Fruit Syrup

Follow the above directions, but pour 1 Tbsp. unsweetened punch powder (like Kool-Aid...any flavor you like) into sugar water in place of the maple flavoring. Stir until well dissolved.

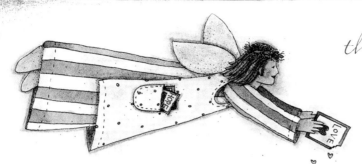

there is nothing half
so sweet in life as
love's young dream.

Clement C. Moore

French Crepes

2 eggs
1/2 cup milk
1/2 cup flour

1 Tbsp. butter
1/2 tsp. vanilla
1/4 tsp. salt

Beat eggs. Melt butter in small skillet. Stir milk, melted butter, vanilla, and salt into eggs. Add flour and beat until creamy. Heat and lightly butter or oil small skillet. Use a measuring cup to pour 1/4 cup of batter into skillet. Quickly swirl pan to spread batter. Cook until edges are brown. Flip crepe and cook other side. Sprinkle with powdered sugar and roll up.

Strawberry-n-Cream Roll-ups

4 oz. cream cheese
1/4 cup powdered sugar
1/2 tsp. vanilla

French crepes
1/2 cup strawberries
1/4 cup sugar

Slice strawberries and sprinkle with sugar. Meanwhile, beat softened cream cheese, powdered sugar, and vanilla together until soft and creamy. Spread cheese mixture and some fresh strawberries on crepes and roll up. Spread more strawberries on top and sprinkle with powdered sugar.

Best-Ever Waffles

1 cup all-purpose flour
1/4 cup sugar
2 tsp. baking powder
1/2 tsp. salt

1/4 cup oil
1 egg
1 cup milk
1/2 tsp. vanilla

Heat waffle iron. Sift dry ingredients together and blend liquid ingredients together. Stir dry ingredients into liquid just until moist. Pour into greased hot waffle iron and close. Cook for 2-3 minutes, or until waffle is golden.

Vanilla Sauce

1/4 cup butter
1/4 cup flour
1/2 cup sugar

1 cup milk
1 tsp. vanilla

Melt butter in saucepan. Stir in flour and sugar. Add milk and cook and stir over medium heat until sauce thickens. Remove from heat and add vanilla.

Banana-Cream Waffles

1 batch waffles   1 batch vanilla sauce   2 bananas

Make waffles and vanilla sauce according to directions. Slice bananas on top of waffles and pour a generous serving of vanilla sauce over bananas and waffles.

teach the young women… to love their husbands   Titus 2:4

Fabulous French Toast

2 eggs
1/4 cup milk
2 Tbsp. flour
3 Tbsp. sugar

1/4 tsp. salt
1/4 tsp. cinnamon
1/2 tsp. vanilla
3-4 thick slices of bread

Beat eggs. Add remaining ingredients except bread and stir vigorously. Dip slices of bread in egg mixture and place on hot buttered griddle. Cook both sides until golden. Sprinkle with powdered sugar. Serve with hot syrup.

Cinnamon-Raisin French Toast

Follow the above recipe, but use cinnamon raisin bread and increase the cinnamon in egg mixture to 1/2 tsp. Serve with Maple-Caramel Sauce.

Maple-Caramel Sauce

2 Tbsp. butter
2 Tbsp. flour
1/2 cup brown sugar

1 cup milk
1 tsp. vanilla
2 Tbsp. maple syrup

Melt butter. Stir in flour and sugar until smooth. Add milk and cook over medium heat, stirring constantly until thickened and bubbly. Add vanilla and maple syrup. Stir well. Yummy on French toast and German pancakes.

Breakfast Dumplings

1 can apple pie filling
1 recipe biscuit dough

*caramel sauce
(opt. whipping cream)

Pour apple pie filling into a pie plate or cake pan. Prepare buttermilk biscuits following recipe on next page. Drop spoonfuls of biscuit dough into apple pie filling. Bake at 400 for 15-20 minutes or until biscuits are golden. Cool slightly before serving. Top with maple-caramel sauce and a dollop of whipped cream.

Crisp-Apple Strudel

1 biscuit recipe
2 crisp apples
3 Tbsp. sugar

3 Tbsp. brown sugar
1 tsp. cinnamon
2 Tbsp. butter

Prepare biscuit dough from recipe on next page. Divide the dough into 2 equal parts. Roll each piece to 1/2" thickness. Core and thinly slice apples. Spread apples evenly down center of dough. Cut butter into small pieces and toss over apples. Mix sugars and cinnamon together and sprinkle over apples. Cut slits in dough 1/2" apart, starting from the edge, cutting upwards on angle until almost reaching the filling. Fold the cut strips down on an angle over the filling, and rotating from side to side, overlapping each time, to weave the strips together. Bake at 350 for 20 minutes or until golden brown. Spread icing on while warm.

Icing: 1 Tbsp. butter   2 tsp. milk   1/2 tsp. vanilla   1/3 cup powdered sugar
Beat butter until soft. Stir in milk, vanilla, and sugar until creamy.

Cinnamon-Crumb Biscuits

1 biscuit recipe
2 Tbsp. sugar
2 Tbsp. brown sugar

1 tsp. cinnamon
1 Tbsp. water
1 icing recipe

Prepare biscuits as below. Form dough into ball. Roll out in a circle on a pizza pan to 3/4" thick. Cut biscuits into squares but don't separate. Mix cinnamon, sugar, and water together until crumbly and spread on biscuits. Bake at 400 for 15-20 min. or until golden brown. Drizzle icing (recipe from previous page) over top while hot.

Buttermilk Biscuits

1 cup flour
2 tsp. baking powder
1/4 tsp. cream of tartar
1/2 tsp. salt

1/4 cup butter
1/3 cup milk
1 tsp. vinegar

Mix vinegar with milk to sour while you sift dry ingredients together. Cut in butter. Add milk and stir just until moist. Roll out on floured surface to about 3/4" thick. Cut biscuits and place on ungreased cookie sheet. Bake at 450 for 10-12 minutes or until golden brown.

Sausage Gravy

1/4 pound pork sausage
2 heaping Tbsp. flour

1 cup milk
salt and pepper

Brown sausage until well done. Stir in flour, milk, salt, and pepper. Cook and stir over medium heat until thickened and bubbly. Serve over biscuits.

Easy Sausage Quiche

1/3 pound pork sausage
3 slices bread
3 eggs

1/2 cup milk
1/2 cup cheese
1/2 tsp. salt

Remove crusts from bread. Tear bread in pieces and spread on bottom of greased pie plate or casserole dish. Cook and drain sausage well. Spread over bread. Sprinkle with cheese. Beat eggs, milk, and salt together. Pour over sausage and cheese. Bake at 350 for 30 minutes.

Quick-n-Easy Hash Browns

You can make hash browns from your baked potatoes. Skin the potatoes and chop or grate into a hot oiled skillet. Sprinkle with salt and pepper and cook over medium heat, turning occasionally, until potatoes start to brown.

Ham Fried Potatoes

2 slices ham
2 small potatoes
2 Tbsp. chopped onion

3 eggs
1/4 cup cheese
salt and pepper

Chop ham into squares. Peel, chop, and rinse potatoes. In a small skillet, saute potatoes and onions in 1 Tbsp. hot oil for 8-9 minutes. Add ham and continue cooking. Beat eggs and pour over ham and potatoes. Sprinkle salt, pepper, and cheese on top. Cook and scramble until eggs are cooked.

Scrambled Eggs

2 to 4 eggs
salt and pepper

1 Tbsp. milk per egg
non-stick cooking spray

Beat eggs with milk. Spray skillet with non-stick cooking spray and place on medium heat. Pour eggs into skillet and sprinkle with salt and pepper. Using a pancake turner, continually fold eggs as they are cooking. Serve with salsa or ketchup.

Deluxe Scrambled Eggs

2 to 4 eggs
1-2 slices of bacon
2 Tbsp. diced green pepper

1/4 cup cheddar cheese
2 Tbsp. chopped onion
salt and pepper

In hot skillet, cook bacon until crispy. Do not drain fat. Crumble bacon into small pieces. Add onions and peppers to skillet. Sauté until onions begin to turn clear. In a mixing bowl, whip eggs and 1 tsp. milk together. Pour eggs into hot skillet. Sprinkle with salt, pepper, and cheese. Using a pancake turner, continually fold eggs while cooking. Serve with salsa or ketchup.

Breakfast Burritos

Prepare eggs according to above directions. Warm flour tortillas in microwave. Place eggs down center of tortillas. Pour salsa over eggs. Roll tortillas.

Ham-n-Cheese and Egg Muffins

2 eggs
2 English muffins

2 slices cheese
2 slices ham

Place a wide-mouth canning jar lid ring on a hot greased skillet. Crack egg and pour into ring. Hold ring down until egg is firm enough that it will not spread outside of the ring. Meanwhile, toast English muffins. Heat ham on skillet. Take ring off egg and turn to cook other side of egg. Place cheese, ham, and egg between muffin halves. Repeat for second egg muffin.

Hard-Boiled Eggs

Place eggs in saucepan. Fill with water to cover eggs. Sprinkle with salt. Bring to a rapid boil. Turn off heat and allow eggs to continue to cook in hot water for 5 minutes. Remove from heat. Run eggs under cold water until you can handle them. Peel shells and rinse eggs. Place in bowls and melt butter on top.

These are great served hot for breakfast with toast and juice.

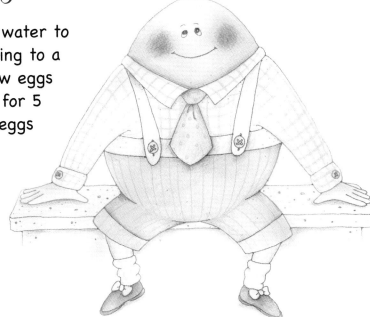

To avoid walking on egg shells ... hard boil your eggs

17

Breakfast Quiche

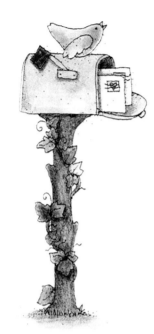

Crust:

1 cup flour	4 Tbsp. butter
1/2 tsp. salt	4 Tbsp. cold water

Sift flour and salt together. Cut in butter. Mix in enough water to form dough. Press dough on bottom of pie plate. (You may use 1 package refrigerator biscuits for crust.)

Quiche Filling:

4 slices crumbled bacon	4 eggs
1/4 cup diced green pepper	1/4 cup cheese
1/4 cup chopped onion	2 Tbsp. milk
1/4 cup chopped tomato	

Sprinkle bacon and vegetables over crust. Whisk eggs, milk, and salt together. Pour egg mixture over vegetables. Sprinkle cheese on top. Bake at 400 for 30 minutes or until knife inserted comes out clean.

Breakfast Omelettes

Using the same ingredients as the quiche recipe, sauté onions and peppers. Beat eggs, milk, and salt together. Pour 1/2 of the egg mixture into a hot oiled small skillet. Cook until brown at edges. Flip over. Sprinkle 1/2 of the sautéed vegetables, bacon, tomatoes, and cheese on top. Cook a few more minutes. Repeat for second omelette. Fold like tacos and serve with salsa.

Veggie-Mushroom ☆ Omelettes

Follow directions for breakfast omelettes but replace bacon with 1/4 cup sauteed mushrooms.

Farmer's Breakfast

2-3 slices ham	4 eggs, well-beaten
1 cup hash-browns	1/4 cup cheese
1/4 cup chopped onion	2 Tbsp. milk

Dice ham into small cubes. Brown ham, hash-browns, and onions in hot skillet until onions are clear and tender. Whip eggs, milk, and cheese together. Pour egg mix into skillet and cook over medium heat, continually folding until eggs are cooked. Serve with salsa or ketchup.

Breakfast Pizza

1 biscuit recipe	deluxe scrambled eggs
1 sausage gravy recipe	1/2 cup cheddar cheese

Prepare biscuit dough according to directions. Roll dough out on pizza pan. Make gravy according to directions. Spread over crust. Make scrambled eggs according to directions and sprinkle over gravy. Top with grated cheese. Bake at 400 for 15-20 minutes or until cheese is melted and bubbly. Slice like a pizza.

Cornbread or Muffins

1/2 cup cornmeal
1/2 cup white or wheat flour
1/2 tsp. salt
3 Tbsp. sugar

2 tsp. baking powder
3 Tbsp. vegetable oil
1 egg (well beaten)
1/2 cup milk

Sift dry ingredients together. Blend egg, oil, and milk together. Stir into dry ingredients just until moist. Pour into greased loaf pan. Bake at 425 for 20-25 minutes or until golden brown.

Cornmeal Muffins: Line or grease a 6 cup muffin pan. Pour batter into cups. Bake at 400 for 12-15 minutes or until golden brown. Try with cranberry or garden cheese spread.

Cranberry Cheese Spread

4 oz. softened cream cheese
2 Tbsp. powdered sugar

1/4 cup dried cranberries
1/2 tsp. vanilla

Mix together cheese, sugar, and vanilla. Fold in dried cranberries. Serve with muffins or bagels.

Garden Cheese Spread

Mix together 4 oz. softened cream cheese, 3 Tbsp. chopped green onions, 1/4 tsp. salt, and 1/2 tsp. Worcestershire sauce. Serve on muffins or bagels.

Applesauce Muffins

3 Tbsp. vegetable oil
1/4 cup applesauce
1/4 cup sugar
1 egg

1/4 cup milk
1 cup flour
1 tsp. baking powder
1/2 tsp. salt

Blend first 5 ingredients. Sift dry ingredients together. Mix the wet and dry ingredients. Fill lined or greased muffin cups 1/2 full. Sprinkle 1 tsp. topping over the batter. Bake at 400 for 15-20 minutes or until golden brown.

Topping: Mix 2 Tbsp. sugar, 2 Tbsp. brown sugar, 1/4 tsp. cinnamon, and 1 Tbsp. water together until mixture is coarse.

Blueberry Muffins

3 Tbsp. vegetable oil
1/2 cup milk
1 egg, well-beaten
3 Tbsp. sugar

1 cup flour
1 1/2 tsp. baking powder
1/2 tsp. salt
1/4 cup blueberries

Mix all ingredients except blueberries together just until moist. Fold in blueberries. Fill lined or greased muffin cups 1/2 full. Bake at 400 for 15-20 minutes or until golden brown. Makes 6 muffins.

You can also make muffins from the bread recipes on the next two pages. Follow baking instructions above with desired batter.

21

Lemon Bread

1/4 cup vegetable oil
1/2 cup sugar
1 egg, well-beaten
1/4 cup milk

3/4 cup flour
1/2 tsp. baking powder
1/4 tsp. salt
1/2 tsp. lemon extract

Blend first 4 ingredients together. Sift dry ingredients together. Mix with egg mixture and stir in lemon extract. Pour into greased loaf pan. Bake at 350 for 30-35 minutes or until knife inserted in center comes out clean. While bread is still hot, prick top all over with ice pick or fork. Pour glaze over top.

Glaze: Stir together 1/4 cup sugar and 1/4 cup lemon juice. Pour over bread. Remove bread from pan when bread is completely cooled.

Banana-Nut Bread

2 medium bananas
1/2 tsp. baking soda
1/4 cup vegetable oil
1/2 cup sugar

1 large egg
3/4 cup flour
1/2 tsp. salt
1/4 cup walnuts (opt.)

Mash bananas with potato masher until all lumps are gone. Dissolve soda in 2 Tbsp. hot water. Add soda to bananas and stir well. Mix all of the remaining ingredients into bananas. Add chopped walnuts if desired. Pour into greased 8x8 cake pan. Bake at 350 for 20-30 minutes or until knife inserted in center comes out clean.

Zucchini Bread

1/3 cup vegetable oil
1 cup chopped zucchini
1 egg
2/3 cup sugar
1 tsp. vanilla

1 cup flour
1/2 tsp. baking soda
1/2 tsp. salt
1 tsp. cinnamon

Blend oil and zucchini in blender until puréed. Add egg and vanilla and blend well. Sift dry ingredients together in a mixing bowl. Pour zucchini mixture in and stir well. Pour into a greased loaf pan. Bake at 350 for 30-35 minutes or until knife inserted comes out clean.

Pumpkin Bread

2/3 cup pumpkin
1/3 cup butter
1 cup sugar
1 large egg

1/2 tsp. vanilla
1/4 cup water
1 1/4 cup flour
1/2 tsp. salt

1/2 tsp. soda
1/2 tsp. nutmeg
1/2 tsp. cinnamon
1/4 tsp. ginger

Cream butter and sugar. Stir in pumpkin and other wet ingredients. Sift together dry ingredients. Add to pumpkin mixture. Stir well. Add chocolate chips, nuts, or raisins. Pour into greased loaf pans. Bake at 350 for 30 minutes or until knife inserted in center comes out clean.

23

Homemade White Bread

1/2 cup milk + 1/2 cup water	2 Tbsp. sugar
1 package active dry yeast	3 1/4 cups flour
2 Tbsp. vegetable oil	1 1/2 tsp. salt

Heat milk in saucepan just until warm. Pour into mixing bowl. Dissolve yeast in 1/2 cup warm water. Add to milk. Stir in oil, sugar, salt, and 2 cups of the flour. Beat at low speed with electric mixer 1 minute, and then on high for 2 minutes. Stir in remaining flour until you can't stir any more. Knead the dough on floured surface, adding flour if needed to make a slightly stiff dough. Place in greased bowl and cover. Put in a warm area to rise (I turn the oven to 200 for a few minutes just to warm it, and then I turn it off before placing the bread inside). Let rise until double (about 1 hour).

Punch the dough down. Roll in flour and shape into loaf. Grease a loaf pan and place dough in pan. Cover and let rise in warm area until almost double in size. Heat oven to 375. Place loaf in oven and bake 30-45 minutes. Remove from pan and place on cooling rack. Tastes yummy served warm with sweet honey butter.

Sweet Honey Butter

1/4 cup honey	2 Tbsp. powdered sugar
3 Tbsp. butter	1/2 tsp. vanilla

Soften butter. Cream together butter and honey. Mix in powdered sugar and vanilla until well blended. Spread over warm bread or scones.

Heavenly Dinner Rolls

1/2 cup warm water
2 tsp. yeast
1/4 cup sugar
1/4 cup butter

1/2 cup milk
1 egg, well-beaten
2 1/2 cups flour
1 tsp. salt

In a mixing bowl, dissolve yeast in warm water. Add sugar to yeast (the sugar will help activate the yeast). Melt butter. Stir milk into melted butter. Add the milk mixture and eggs to yeast. Stir in enough flour to make a stiff dough. Knead 5-7 minutes on floured surface. Place in greased bowl and put in warm place to rise. Let rise about 30 minutes. Punch dough down. Shape rolls. Place in warm area and let rise 30 minutes. Bake at 400 for 12-15 minutes or until golden brown. Place on cooling rack and brush butter over tops of rolls.

Crescent Rolls (my favorite!): Roll dough into a circle about 1/2" thick. Cut as you would a pizza into 8-12 wedges. Starting at outside edge, roll dough to pointed end. Place on greased baking sheet, point down and curve ends a little to look like a crescent moon. Follow above directions for raising and baking.

Parker House Rolls: Roll out dough to 1/2" thick-ness. Cut dough into 12 squares. Fold squares in half and place on greased baking sheet. Follow above directions for raising and baking.

She who bakes bread...has warm hands and a warm heart!

Honey-Wheat Bread

1 cup warm water
1 package active dry yeast
1 Tbsp. vegetable oil
1 1/2 Tbsp. honey

1 tsp. salt
1/2 tsp. wheat gluten
3 cups whole wheat flour

Dissolve yeast in warm water. Stir in oil, honey, salt, gluten, and 2 cups of flour. Beat at low speed with electric mixer 1 minute, and then on high for 2 minutes. Stir in remaining flour until you can't stir any more. Knead the dough on floured surface, adding flour if needed to make a slightly stiff dough. Place in greased bowl and cover. Put in a warm area to rise (about 1 1/2 hours).
Punch dough down. Roll in flour and shape into loaf. Grease a loaf pan and place dough in pan. Cover and let rise in warm area until almost double in size. Heat oven to 375. Place loaf in oven and bake 30-45 minutes. Remove from pan.

Honey-Wheat Rolls

1/2 cup warm water
2 tsp. yeast
1/4 cup sugar
1/4 cup butter

1/2 cup milk
1 egg, well-beaten
2 1/2 cups flour
1 tsp. salt

Dissolve yeast in warm water. Melt butter. Stir melted butter and remaining ingredients into yeast. Stir until smooth. Knead 5-7 minutes, adding enough flour to make a moderately stiff dough. Place in greased bowl and put in a warm place to rise. Let rise about 45 minutes. Punch dough down. Shape rolls. Place in warm area and let rise 45 minutes. Bake at 400 for 12-15 minutes or until golden brown. Place on cooling rack and brush butter over tops of rolls.

Breadsticks or Scones

Follow the wheat or white bread recipe, but instead of shaping into loaf, roll dough to 1/2" thickness.

Breadsticks: Cut 2" strips and place on greased baking sheet. Let rise until double. Brush with milk. Bake at 400 for 15-20 minutes or until golden brown.

Parmesan Breadsticks: Follow directions for breadsticks, but remove from oven at 7 minutes. Brush with butter and sprinkle Parmesan cheese on top. Continue baking for an additional 7-10 minutes.

Scones: Cut 3" squares. Pour oil 1" deep in a skillet and turn heat to medium temperature. Place a match in the oil. When the oil is hot enough, the match will light. Remove the match. Stretch scones and place in oil. Cook until edges start to turn golden. Turn and cook on other side. Place scone on paper towel to absorb excess oil. Serve with sweet honey butter or jam.

Aunt Julie's Cinnamon Roll-Up

Roll dough out into a rectangle 1/2" thick. Sprinkle a few drops of water on dough and use your hand to spread it around until dough is sticky. Blend 1/4 cup sugar and 1 tsp. cinnamon together and sprinkle over sticky dough. Roll up dough. Using a sharp knife, cut slits 1/2" apart down through the dough. Gently push rolled slices over to one side to look like collapsed dominoes. Bake at 350 for 30-35 minutes or until done. Drizzle icing on top. (Recipe for icing is with Crisp Apple Strudel recipe.)

French Bread

1 cup warm water	1 Tbsp. white vinegar
1 package active dry yeast	3-4 cups bread flour
1 Tbsp. sugar	1 1/2 tsp. salt
1/4 cup vegetable oil	1 egg white, slightly beaten

Dissolve yeast in water. Stir in sugar, oil, vinegar, salt, and 2 cups of the flour. Beat at low speed with electric mixer 1 minute, and then on high for 2 minutes. Stir in flour until you can't stir any more. Knead dough on floured surface. Place dough in a greased bowl and cover and let rise until double. Punch dough down. Roll dough to 9"x 12". Roll up to be 9"x 4". Place on greased baking sheet and brush top with egg white. Cut 3 slits diagonally across top of loaf. Let rise in warm area 30 minutes. Bake at 400 for 30-35 minutes or until golden brown. (You can also sprinkle sesame seeds on top before baking.)

Garlic Bread

Garlic Bread: Cut slices of French bread and place open-face on baking sheet. Spread butter on each slice. Sprinkle salt, garlic powder, and Parmesan cheese on each slice. Broil 3-4 minutes or until cheese starts to brown.

friendship... like Yeast, needs a warm place to grow.

Mashed Potato Rolls

1/4 cup warm water
2 tsp. yeast
3 Tbsp. sugar
1/4 cup butter
1/2 cup mashed potatoes

1 egg, well-beaten
1/2 cup warm milk
3-4 cups flour
1/2 tsp. salt

Dissolve yeast in warm water. Melt butter. Blend milk, butter, salt, sugar, potatoes, and egg in mixing bowl. Stir in yeast. Stir in flour until you can't stir any more. Turn onto floured surface and knead dough, adding flour until dough is stiff. Place in greased bowl and let rise until double. Punch down. Shape into rolls and place on greased baking sheet. Allow to rise. Bake at 350 for 15-18 minutes.

Fried Bread

1 cup wheat or white flour
2 tsp. baking powder

1/2 tsp. salt
water

Mix dry ingredients together. Slowly stir in water until stiff dough forms. Pull off pieces and stretch into 5" circles. Fry bread in hot oil, turning to cook both sides. Place on paper towel to drain excess oil. Tastes great with honey or jam. Serve these with refried beans and toppings for Navajo Tacos.

In Just 5 Minutes - Hot Oatmeal

1/2 cup quick oats
1 cup water
milk or cream

1/4 cup sugar
1/4 tsp. salt

Boil salt and water. Stir in the oats and sugar. Turn off heat and let sit for a few minutes. Serve with milk or cream.

Maple-Nut Oatmeal

Follow the Hot Oatmeal directions but replace sugar with brown sugar and add 1/4 cup walnuts and 1/4 tsp. maple flavoring. Serve with milk or cream.

Cinnamon-Raisin Oatmeal

Follow Hot Oatmeal directions but replace sugar with brown sugar and add 1/4 cup raisins and 1/2 teaspoon cinnamon. Serve with milk or cream.

Strawberries-n-Cream Oatmeal

Follow Hot Oatmeal directions but stir in *strawberry topping after oatmeal is cooked. Serve with milk or cream.

Stove-Top Granola

3 Tbsp. butter
3 Tbsp. milk
1/4 cup sugar
1/4 cup brown sugar

3 Tbsp. peanut butter
1/4 cup raisins
1/2 tsp. vanilla
2-3 cups quick oats

Melt butter. Stir in milk and sugars. Bring to a boil and continue stirring for 2 more minutes. Remove from heat and stir in peanut butter and vanilla. Stir in oats to desired texture.

For crispy granola, spread on a cookie sheet and broil 3-4 minutes in oven.
For chocolate chip granola, substitute chocolate chips for raisins.

Fruit and Yogurt Parfaits

2 cups plain yogurt
1/4 powdered sugar
1/2 tsp. vanilla

1 cup frozen mixed fruit
2 Tbsp. sugar
granola

Stir yogurt, powdered sugar, and vanilla together.
In separate bowl, stir sugar and fruit together.
Layer yogurt and fruit in mug or dessert glass.
Sprinkle granola over top.

A friend is a second self.

Aristotle

Baked Rice Pudding

1 cup cooked rice
3/4 cup milk
1/3 cup sugar
1 tsp. cinnamon

1/2 tsp. salt
3 eggs, well-beaten
1/2 tsp. vanilla
1/3 cup raisins

Mix rice, milk, eggs, and vanilla together in a small casserole dish. Blend sugar, cinnamon, and salt together. Add cinnamon mixture to rice mixture. Stir well. Fold in raisins. Bake at 350 for 30 minutes. Stir pudding and bake an additional 10-15 minutes or until firm. Rice pudding can be served as a dessert or served with milk as a cereal.

Cracked Wheat Cereal

1/2 cup cracked wheat
1 cup water
milk or cream

3 Tbsp. sugar
1/2 tsp. salt

You can buy cracked wheat cereal in the grocery store. It is usually in the same area as the oatmeal. Or you can crack wheat in your blender. Put the amount of wheat needed in blender and blend on high. Boil water and salt. Stir in wheat and sugar. Reduce heat and simmer about 5 minutes. Serve in bowls with milk or cream.

My Favorite Recipes

No Success can compensate for FAILURE in the HOME   David O. McKay

My Favorite Recipes

_____
_____
_____
_____
_____
_____
_____
_____
_____
_____
_____
_____
_____
_____
_____
_____
_____
_____
_____
_____
_____
_____
_____
_____

Let's Do Lunch

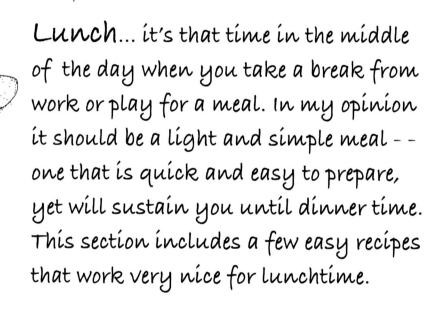

Let's Do Lunch

Lunch... it's that time in the middle of the day when you take a break from work or play for a meal. In my opinion it should be a light and simple meal -- one that is quick and easy to prepare, yet will sustain you until dinner time. This section includes a few easy recipes that work very nice for lunchtime.

Also included in this section are some ideas for using your leftovers. You will find the recipes at the end of this section.

Veggie Wraps

2-4 tortillas (recipe below) tomato slices red onion slices
2 slices mozzarella cheese green peppers avocados
cucumber slices lettuce black olives

Prepare tortillas from recipe below. Slice or chop vegetables. Layer cheese and vegetables in tortilla and wrap up burrito style.

Tortillas: 1 cup wheat or white flour 2 Tbsp. vegetable oil
      1 tsp. baking powder 1/3 cup water
      1/2 tsp. salt

Sift dry ingredients together. Mix in oil and stir until crumbly. Add water and stir until stiff dough forms. Knead lightly. Separate into 4 balls. Roll each ball until thin like a tortilla. Cook 2-3 minutes on each side on lightly oiled griddle.

Grilled Chicken Wraps

1 boneless chicken breast 2 Tbsp. fajita seasoning
1/3 cup diced green pepper 1/2 cup grated cheese
1/4 cup diced onion sour cream
1 tomato, chopped salsa

Cut chicken into 1" strips. In a skillet, sauté peppers and onions in 1 tsp. oil until tender. Remove from skillet. Cook chicken in 1 tsp. hot oil until outside becomes white. Reduce heat. Add fajita seasoning and 1/4 cup water. Cover and simmer 15 minutes. Return vegetables to skillet. Add tomatoes and warm through. Warm tortillas. Wrap with fajita mix, cheese, sour cream, and salsa.

Did you have meatloaf and baked potatoes for dinner last night? ...if so, here are a few recipes to make use of the leftovers.

Mom's Meatloaf Sandwiches

2 slices leftover meatloaf   mayonnaise or salad dressing
4 slices whole wheat bread

Slice 2 thick slices of leftover meatloaf. Spread salad dressing on bread. Place meatloaf between slices. Tastes great with baked potato salad.

You can also warm the meatloaf and serve it on a bun with lettuce, tomatoes, pickles, and other toppings as you would a hamburger.

Baked Potato Salad

2 baked potatoes (warm)   1/3 cup cheddar cheese
1 finely diced green onion   1/3 cup ranch dressing

Warm leftover baked potatoes. Peel and chop potatoes. Mix potatoes, onions, cheese, and ranch dressing together. Serve while still warm.

Bacon Baked-Potato Salad

Follow recipe for Baked Potato Salad but add 1/3 cup cooked and crumbled bacon bits. Serve warm.

Sweet-n-Sour Meatloaf Bites

1/4 cup sugar
1/4 cup brown sugar
2 Tbsp. ketchup
2 Tbsp. mustard
1/4 cup barbecue sauce

1/4 cup apple cider vinegar
1/4 cup water
1 tsp. cornstarch
2 Tbsp. chili sauce (opt.)
Leftover meatloaf

Mix sugars, ketchup, mustard, sauces, and vinegar in saucepan. Stir cornstarch into water. Add to saucepan. Cook and stir over medium heat until thickened. Remove from heat. Cut meatloaf into 1" cubes. Add meatloaf bites to sauce. Continue to cook until meatloaf bites are warmed through. Serve over steamed rice.

Steamed Rice

1 cup long-grain rice
2 cups water

1 Tbsp. butter
1/2 tsp. salt

Bring the two cups water to a boil. Add rice, salt, and butter and stir well. Reduce temperature to medium-low and place a tight-fitting lid on pan. Simmer 20 minutes. Remove from heat and fluff with fork. Serve while still warm.

Bean and Cheese Burritos

2 flour tortillas
1/2 cup canned refried beans

1/4 cup grated cheese
sour cream and salsa

Warm tortillas on hot griddle or skillet. Spread about 1/4 cup refried beans on each tortilla. Sprinkle 2 Tbsp. cheese over beans. Fold sides over beans and roll tortilla up. Cook both sides until hot and slightly crispy. Spread salsa and sour cream on top. Serve with a bed of shredded lettuce, chopped tomatoes, onions, and peppers. These are also great with guacamole.

Stack Enchiladas

4 corn tortillas
1/2 lb. hamburger
1/2 can refried beans
4 oz. enchilada sauce

1/2 cup grated cheese
sour cream and salsa
toppings
guacamole (opt.)

Brown hamburger with salt, pepper, and garlic powder. Warm enchilada sauce and beans in separate pans. Chop toppings such as lettuce, tomatoes, onions, peppers, and olives. Dip tortillas one at a time into enchilada sauce. Place on plate. Spread beans and meat over entire enchilada. Sprinkle cheese, toppings, sour cream, salsa, and guacamole on top. Dip second tortilla in sauce and place on top. Repeat layer of toppings. Pour extra enchilada sauce on top if desired.

Guacamole: Mash 1 avocado. Mix with 1/4 tsp. salt and 1/4 tsp. lemon juice.

Taco Salad

About 20 corn tortilla chips
1 cup torn lettuce leaves
1/2 can kidney beans
1/2 can whole-kernel corn
1/4 cup chopped bell pepper
1/2 cup chopped cucumber

1/2 cup chopped tomato
1/3 cup sliced olives
1/2 cup grated cheese
ranch dressing
salsa

Warm kidney beans. Break up 6-10 tortilla chips into each bowl. Toss desired amount of remaining ingredients over chips in order listed. Pour salad dressing and salsa over top.

Quesadillas

2-4 flour tortillas   1/4-1/2 cup grated cheddar cheese

Warm one side of each tortilla on hot griddle or in hot skillet. Turn over and sprinkle 2 Tbsp. grated cheese on warmed side of each tortilla. Fold tortilla in half and cook both sides until hot and slightly crispy.

Spicy Quesadillas

Follow above directions, but sprinkle 1 Tbsp. diced green chilies and 1 tsp. Tapatio hot sauce with cheese. Cook as above.

A soft voice turneth away wrath.
Howard W. Hunter

41

Egg Salad Sandwiches

4 hard-cooked eggs	paprika
1/4 cup salad dressing	salt and pepper
1 tsp. mustard	lettuce leaves
4 bread slices	

Peel and rinse eggs. Mash in bowl and mix with salad dressing, mustard, salt, pepper, and paprika. Spread on 2 slices of bread. Top with lettuce leaves and remaining 2 slices of bread. Cut in half. Serve with tomato wedges or slices.

Tuna Salad Sandwiches

1 can tuna	1/4 cup chopped tomato
3 Tbsp. salad dressing	2 Tbsp. chopped dill pickles
1/2 tsp. mustard	1/4 cup chopped lettuce
4 bread slices	

Mix all ingredients. Spread on 2 slices of bread. Top with remaining bread slices. Cut sandwiches in half. Serve with celery and carrot sticks and potato chips.

You can substitute chicken or turkey for the tuna to make chicken or turkey salad sandwiches.

Tuna Melts

1 can tuna
3 Tbsp. salad dressing
2-4 slices mozzarella cheese

1 tomato, sliced
2-4 slices bread

Lightly toast bread. Put slices of toast on baking sheet. Mix tuna with salad dressing. Spread over toast. Lay tomato on tuna and place a slice of cheese on top of tomato. Broil until cheese melts. Tastes great served with pickles.

Ham-and-Cheese Pockets

6-8 refrigerator biscuits
3-4 slices cheddar cheese

3-4 slices ham

You will use two biscuits for each ham and cheese pocket. Spray baking sheet with cooking spray. Press biscuits flat and place half of them on baking sheet. Cut ham and cheese slices to be 1/2" smaller than biscuits. Layer one slice of ham and cheese on top of one biscuit and place another biscuit on top. Pinch edges together to seal. Repeat for remaining biscuits. Cut 2-3 slits in top. Bake at 400 for 10-12 minutes.

43

Macaroni and Cheese

1 cup macaroni noodles   2 Tbsp. butter
3/4 cup cheddar cheese   1/4 cup milk

Cook noodles according to package directions. Drain noodles and return to pan. Melt butter into noodles. Add milk and grated cheese. Stir until cheese melts. Season with salt to taste.

Tomato-Macaroni Bake

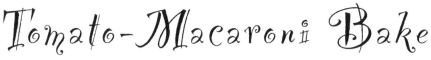

Make the above recipe and turn into casserole dish.

Add the following:

    1 cup diced fresh or canned tomatoes
    1 cup whole-kernel corn

Mix well and sprinkle with salt and pepper. Bake at 400 for 10 minutes.

Chili-Macaroni

Follow above directions, but add 1/2 cup sour cream and 1 can chili con carne in place of tomatoes. Mix well. Sprinkle extra cheddar cheese on top. Bake 15-20 minutes at 350.

We always have leftover spaghetti noodles and sauce. If you have the same problem, try these quick and tasty recipes.

Spaghetti Salad

1 cup cooked noodles
1/3 cup Italian dressing
1/2 cup chopped tomato
1/2 cup chopped cucumber

2 Tbsp. chopped green pepper
2 Tbsp. chopped red onion
1/2 cup sliced ripe olives
2 Tbsp. Parmesan cheese

Mix all ingredients except Parmesan cheese together until everything is well-coated with dressing. Sprinkle Parmesan cheese on top when serving.

Baked Spaghetti

1-2 cups cooked noodles
1 cup spaghetti sauce

1/2 cup mozzarella cheese
3 Tbsp. Parmesan cheese

Mix noodles, sauce, and mozzarella cheese in a casserole dish. Bake at 350 for 10 minutes. Sprinkle Parmesan cheese on top and bake 5 more minutes.

Pizza Burgers

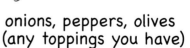

2-4 slices bread or buns
spaghetti sauce
1/2 cup mozzarella cheese

onions, peppers, olives
(any toppings you have)

Toast tops of bread or buns using the broiler in your oven. Spread sauce over top of bun. Sprinkle cheese and any toppings desired. Broil 3-4 minutes.

Cabbage-Parmesan Pasta

1 cup sliced cabbage
3 slices chopped bacon
1/4 cup chopped onion

1 shredded carrot
Parmesan cheese
1 cup egg noodles

Cook bacon until well done in a skillet. Add vegetables and sauté until tender. Meanwhile, cook noodles according to package directions. Drain and add to skillet. Serve with Parmesan cheese sprinkled on top.

Italian Pasta Salad

1 cup chopped broccoli
1/2 cup frozen peas
1/4 cup Italian dressing

1 cup curly noodles
Parmesan cheese

Cook noodles according to package directions. Drain and place in bowl. Mix remaining ingredients together. Serve cold.

Tuna-Pasta Salad

1 cup salad pasta noodles
1/3 cup salad dressing
1 can tuna
1 tsp. mustard
2 Tbsp. chopped onion

2 Tbsp. chopped celery
1 chopped dill pickle
1/2 cup frozen peas
2 hard-boiled eggs

Cook noodles according to directions. Mix remaining ingredients except eggs and peas. Stir in noodles until well coated. Peel and chop eggs. Fold in eggs and peas. You can use cooked chicken or turkey in place of tuna.

Lettuce Wraps

5-6 large lettuce leaves
(iceberg works great)

1 recipe tuna, chicken, or egg salad

You can make lettuce wraps by using washed leaves of lettuce and a tuna, chicken, or egg salad recipe. Spread salad mix of your choice down center of lettuce and wrap up lettuce like a tortilla. These taste crisp, fresh, and delicious.

You can also make lettuce wraps using hot foods inside. Stir-fried chicken and vegetable or rice recipes as well as Mexican rice and beans are very delicious in a lettuce wrap.

Chicken Caesar Wraps

2-3 tortillas
1/2 cup cooked chicken

1 cup bagged Caesar salad mix
Caesar dressing

Combine chicken, salad mix, and dressing in bowl. Warm tortillas in micowave or on a griddle. Place chicken mix in tortillas and wrap. Serve warm or cold. (If serving warm, heat chicken through before mixing with other ingredients.)

Bowtie Chicken Salad

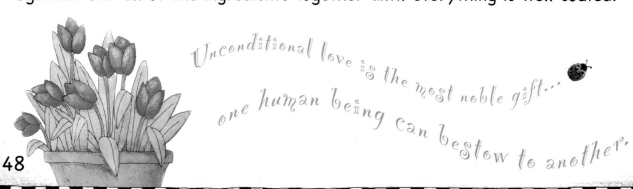

1/2 cup bowtie pasta
1/2 cup rainbow pasta
1/2 cup cooked chicken
1/2 cup pineapple tidbits
1/2 cup red grapes

1 celery rib
1 green onion
1/2 cup craisins
3 Tbsp. sugar
1/3 cup mayonnaise

Cook rainbow and bowtie pasta according to package directions. Drain and cool pasta. Pour pineapple into strainer to drain juice. Meanwhile, cut grapes in half lengthwise. Chop chicken, celery, and green onions. Mix sugar and mayonnaise together. Stir all of the ingredients together until everything is well coated.

Unconditional love is the most noble gift... one human being can bestow to another.

Chicken Lo Mein

1 cup spaghetti noodles	1 rib celery, sliced
1 chicken breast	1 Tbsp. cornstarch
1 carrot, peeled and sliced	1/2 tsp. ginger
1/2 cup chopped broccoli	1 Tbsp. soy sauce
2 Tbsp. chopped onion	2 Tbsp. vegetable oil

Cook noodles according to directions. Cut chicken into 1" strips and chop the vegetables. Heat 1 Tbsp. oil in skillet. Sauté vegetables until tender. Remove from skillet. Heat remaining oil. Add chicken and cook just until edges are browned. Add 1/4 cup water and ginger to chicken and simmer 4-5 minutes. Stir cornstarch into 1/4 cup cold water. Add cornstarch to skillet. Cook and stir over medium heat until thickened and bubbly. Return the vegetables to skillet and heat through. Stir in soy sauce and noodles.

☆Oriental Chicken Salad

1 cup mixed salad greens	1/2 cup mandarin oranges
1/2 cup chow mein noodles	1/4 cup sliced almonds
1/2 cup chopped cooked chicken	Sesame Dressing

Tear greens and place on two plates. Sprinkle remaining ingredients on top.

Sesame Dressing: Mix together 2 Tbsp. sugar, 1 Tbsp. vinegar, 2 Tbsp. oil, 1/4 tsp. salt, and 1 Tbsp. sesame seeds. Stir until sugar dissolves. Pour over salad.

Macaroni and Cheese Salad

1 cup salad-roni (ditalini)
1/2 cup salad dressing
1/2 cup chopped dill pickles

1/2 cup cheddar cheese
1/2 cup sliced olives
1 Tbsp. mustard (opt.)

Cook noodles according to package directions. Meanwhile, cut cheese into 1/2" cubes and mix with remaining ingredients. Stir noodles into salad. Sprinkle with salt and pepper.

Mashed Potato Salad

3 cooked potatoes
3 hard-boiled eggs
1 chopped dill pickle
1/4 cup chopped onion

1/3 cup salad dressing
2 tsp. mustard
salt and pepper
paprika

Boil potatoes in salted water until tender. Peel and let cool. Mix salad dressing, mustard, salt, pepper, pickles, and onions together. Peel and chop 2 eggs. Grate potatoes. Stir in grated potatoes and chopped eggs. Slice remaining egg and place on salad. Sprinkle with paprika.

Debbie G. Harman

Rainbow Garden Pasta

1 cup rainbow pasta
1/2 cup chopped cauliflower
1/2 cup chopped broccoli
2 Tbsp. chopped red onion

1/2 cup sliced olives
1/4 cup chopped pepper
1/4 cup chopped tomatoes
1/4 cup Italian dressing

Cook pasta according to package directions. Mix all of the vegetables together with the dressing and allow to marinate while the pasta is cooking. Drain pasta and allow to cool. Fold pasta into salad.

Carrot-Raisin Salad

1 cup grated carrots
3 Tbsp. salad dressing

1/4 cup raisins

Peel and grate enough carrots to make 1 cup. Combine with salad dressing and raisins. Allow to sit a few minutes before serving.

Time spent with a true friend... is nourishment for the soul.

Unknown

My Favorite Recipes

_____
_____
_____
_____
_____
_____
_____
_____
_____
_____
_____
_____
_____
_____
_____
_____
_____
_____
_____
_____
_____
_____
_____

No Success can compensate for FAILURE in the HOME   David O. McKay

Soups and Stews

Soups and Stews

Nothing warms the soul on a cold day like a bowl of hot soup. The next few pages are filled with some of the most comforting recipes that are easy to make and easy on the budget, too!

Most of the recipes are made in a crockpot, but you can simmer them in a pot on the stove if you do not have a crockpot.

The bread recipes that are suggested to go with the soups can be found in the Breakfast to Brunch section.

Corn Chowder

1/2 onion, chopped
1 Tbsp. butter
1 potato, chopped
1 cup water
1 cup milk

1 heaping Tbsp. flour
1/2 cup corn
1/2 tsp. salt
dash pepper

Sauté onion in butter in saucepan until tender and clear. Add potatoes and water. Simmer 20 minutes or until potatoes are tender. Gradually stir milk into flour. Stir flour mixture, corn, salt, and pepper into potatoes. Bring soup to a boil, stirring constantly. Reduce heat and simmer 10 minutes.

Creamy Broccoli Soup

2 potatoes, peeled and chopped
1 broccoli stalk, chopped
1 carrot, peeled and grated
1 cup water

1 chicken bouillon cube
1/2 can cream of chicken soup
1/2 cup sour cream

In saucepan, dissolve bouillon cube in water. Layer potatoes, broccoli, and carrots in that order in pan, sprinkling a little salt over each layer. Cover and simmer 20 minutes or until broccoli is tender but not mushy. Turn off heat. Mash vegetables lightly with potato masher. Stir in soup and sour cream. Yummy with cornbread.

For thou shalt eat the labour of thine hands;
happy shalt thou be,
and it shall be well with thee.

Psalms 128: 2

Cheesy Vegetable Chowder

1/4 cup onion, diced
1 carrot, peeled and diced
1 potato, peeled and cubed
1/2 cup cauliflower, chopped
1 cup water
1 cube chicken bouillon

1/2 cup broccoli, chopped
1/2 tsp. salt
1 cup milk
2 Tbsp. flour
1/2 cup cheddar cheese
1/4 cup sour cream

Simmer vegetables except broccoli in bouillon/water until carrots are tender. Add broccoli and salt and simmer 10 more minutes. Slowly stir milk into flour until well mixed. Stir flour mixture into vegetable broth. Cook over medium heat, stirring constantly until soup thickens and begins to boil. Reduce heat. Add grated cheese and sour cream. Cook and stir until cheese is melted.

Cheesy Bacon-Vegetable Chowder

Cook bacon until crisp. Crumble bacon. Using above recipe, add water, bouillon, and vegetables to bacon. Continue by following above directions.

New England Clam Chowder

2 slices bacon, cut up
1 6-1/2 oz. can minced clams
2 potatoes, peeled and diced
1/4 cup chopped onions
1/4 cup finely diced celery

1 heaping Tbsp. flour
1 cup milk
1/2 cup canned milk
1/4 tsp. Worcestershire
    sauce

Cook bacon pieces in medium saucepan until crisp. Drain clams, reserving liquid. Add water to clam juice to make 1 cup liquid. Add liquid and vegetables to the cooked bacon. Cover and simmer 20 minutes or until potatoes are tender. Stir milk slowly into flour. Add flour mixture and clams to soup. Cook and stir over medium heat until thickened and bubbly. Add canned milk and Worcestershire sauce. Sprinkle with salt and pepper.

Potato Chowder

Follow the above directions, but increase bacon to four slices and replace clams with one peeled and grated carrot.

Ham-n-Potato Chowder: Follow recipe, but substitute 1/2 cup chopped ham for bacon.

Cheesy Potato Chowder: Add 1/2 cup grated cheddar cheese to potato chowder recipe.

Chicken and Rice Soup

1/2 lb. chicken (with skin and bone)	2 carrots, sliced
1 rib celery (whole)	1/2 onion, chopped
1/2 onion (whole piece)	1 rib celery, sliced
1/2 tsp. salt	1 cup cooked rice
1/4 tsp. tarragon	1/2 tsp. parsley
2 cups water	salt and pepper

Place chicken and next five ingredients in pot. Bring to a boil. Reduce heat and simmer 1 hour or until chicken pulls away from bone. Strain broth and remove bones and skin from chicken. Throw away skin, bones, and vegetables. Return broth to pot. Add the cut vegetables, parsley, salt, and pepper and simmer 20 minutes. Add cooked rice and simmer 15 minutes. Meanwhile, cube chicken meat. Add chicken to pot and simmer 5 minutes.

Homemade Egg Noodles

1 small egg, well-beaten	1/4 tsp. salt
1 Tbsp. milk	1/2 cup flour

Combine egg, milk, and salt in a mixing bowl. Stir in flour until a stiff dough forms. Cover and let rest 10 minutes. Roll out very thin. Allow dough to dry about 20 more minutes. Roll up the dough loosely and cut strips 1/4" to 1/2" through the entire roll. Carefully unroll strips and cut to desired lengths. Drop into boiling salted water or soup. Cook, uncovered, 10-12 minutes.

Chicken Noodle Soup

1 lb. chicken (with skin and bone)
1 rib celery (whole)
1/2 onion (whole piece)
1/2 tsp. salt
1/4 tsp. tarragon
2 cups water

2 carrots, sliced
1/2 onion, chopped
1 rib celery, sliced
1 cup egg noodles
1/2 tsp. parsley
salt and pepper

Place chicken and next five ingredients in pot. Bring to a boil. Reduce heat and simmer 1 hour or until chicken pulls away from bone. Strain broth and remove bones and skin from chicken. Throw away skin, bones, and vegetables. Return broth to pot. Add the cut vegetables, parsley, salt, and pepper and simmer 20 minutes. Add noodles and simmer 10 minutes. Meanwhile, cube chicken meat. Add chicken to pot and simmer 5 minutes.

Cheesy Chicken Soup

2 potatoes, chopped
2 carrots, chopped
2 cups water
1 chicken bouillon cube
1 cup chopped broccoli

2 ribs celery, chopped
1/4 cup chopped onion
1 can cream of chicken soup
1/2 cup grated cheese
1/2 cup cooked chicken

Steam carrots and potatoes together until soft. Mash by hand. Dissolve bouillon cube in 2 cups water in soup pot. Add onions, celery, and broccoli. Simmer 20 minutes. Stir everything together and heat through until cheese melts.

Hearty Beef Stew

1 Tbsp. all-purpose flour
1/2 lb. beef stew meat
1 Tbsp. vegetable oil
1/4 tsp. garlic powder
1/2 cup chopped onion
1 beef bouillon cube

1 12-oz. can V-8 juice
1/2 cup water
1 potato, peeled and cubed
1 celery rib, sliced
1 carrot, peeled and sliced
salt and pepper

Put flour and 1/2 tsp. salt in a quart-size zip-top bag. Cut stew meat into 1" cubes. Shake meat pieces in bag to coat. Heat oil in medium saucepan. Brown stew meat a few pieces at a time. Add garlic powder, onion, bouillon, V-8, and water. Bring to a boil. Reduce heat, cover, and simmer about 1 hour or until meat is tender. Stir in potatoes, celery, and carrots. Cover and simmer 30 minutes.

Vegetable Beef Soup

Follow recipe for beef stew, but increase water to 2 cups and add another beef bouillon cube. Replace V-8 juice with 1 tomato, peeled and chopped, 1/2 cup whole-kernel corn, 1/4 cup green beans, and 1/4 cup peas.

The better part of one's life...
consists of his friendships.
Abraham Lincoln

Minestrone Soup

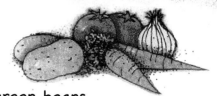

1/4 cup diced onion
1 rib celery, sliced
1 carrot, peeled and diced
3/4 cup water
1 bay leaf
1 10-oz. can tomato soup

1/2 cup green beans
1/4 cup cooked garbanzo beans
1/4 tsp. garlic powder
1/2 tsp. parsley
salt and pepper

Pour water into medium saucepan. Add onions, celery, carrots, bay leaf, and other seasonings. Simmer 20 minutes or until carrots are tender. Stir in the remaining ingredients and simmer 5 more minutes. Remove and discard bay leaf. Serve with cornbread.

Soup is a great way to meet your veggie quota for the day!

Mushroom-Onion Soup

2 Tbsp. butter
1/2 onion, sliced
1/2 cup mushrooms
1 heaping Tbsp. flour

1 beef bouillon cube
1 cup water
1/4 cup half-and-half
1/2 cup cooked rice

In a medium saucepan, sauté onions and mushrooms in butter until onions start to brown. Dissolve bouillon in water to make broth. Slowly stir broth into flour. Add broth to sautéed vegetables. Cook and stir over medium heat until broth boils and thickens. Add half-and-half and rice. Stir well and warm through.

Hamburger Soup

1/2 lb. hamburger
2 cups water
1 beef bouillon cube
1/4 cup chopped onion
1 carrot, chopped
1 celery rib, sliced

1 potato, peeled and chopped
1/4 tsp. celery salt
1/8 tsp. basil
1/2 cup whole-kernel corn
salt and pepper

Brown hamburger and drain fat. Place water, bouillon, onions, carrots, celery, potatoes, and seasonings in stock pot. Bring to a boil. Reduce heat and simmer 20 minutes or until carrots are tender. Add hamburger and corn and simmer 10 more minutes. Season with salt and pepper. Serve with breadsticks.

Snowflake Soup

leftover hamburger soup
water
1 beef bouillon cube
oyster crackers

Pour leftover soup in saucepan. Add enough water to make two cups broth. Stir in bouillon cube until it dissolves. Warm through. When serving, sprinkle several oyster crackers over soup.

(The crackers are the snowflakes!)

Creamy Hamburger Soup

1/2 lb. hamburger
1 cup canned tomatoes
   (with juice)
1/2 cup water
1 bay leaf
1/4 tsp. marjoram

1 potato, peeled and grated
1 carrot, peeled and grated
1/2 can cream of mushroom soup
1/2 cup sour cream
salt and pepper

Brown hamburger. Drain fat. Pour tomatoes and water into medium saucepan. Bring to a boil. Reduce heat. Add seasonings, potatoes, and carrots and simmer until vegetables are tender. Remove bay leaf. Add soup and sour cream and stir well. Serve with French bread or hard rolls.

Tomato Soup

1 1/2 cups water
1 chicken bouillon cube
4 fresh tomatoes, skinned
1/4 cup chopped onion
1 celery rib, chopped

1 Tbsp. parsley flakes
1/4 tsp. garlic powder
2 Tbsp. butter
1 heaping Tbsp. flour

Chop tomatoes. Bring tomatoes and water to boil in medium saucepan. Reduce heat. Add vegetables, bouillon, and seasonings and simmer 20 minutes. Remove from heat. Pour into blender and blend on high until pureed. Meanwhile, melt butter in saucepan. Add flour and mix well. Slowly stir in tomato puree. Cook on medium heat, stirring constantly until soup thickens.

Easy Taco Soup

1/2 lb. hamburger
1 Tbsp. taco seasoning
1 can chili con carne
1/2 cup whole-kernel corn
1 can vegetable soup

1/2 cup mild salsa
1/2 cup water
corn tortilla chips
sour cream, cheese,
   and other toppings

Brown hamburger and drain fat. Mix meat with next six ingredients. Simmer 20-30 minutes. Serve over chips and top with sour cream, cheese, and other toppings of choice (lettuce, olives, peppers, etc.).

Lori's Tortilla Stew

1 chicken breast (with bone and skin)
1 cup water
1 chicken bouillon cube
1/2 tsp. paprika
1 can Mexican stewed tomatoes
1 sm. can diced green chilies
1/4 cup diced onions

1/2 tsp. salt
1 tsp. chili powder
1/2 tsp. garlic powder
tortilla chips
Monterey Jack cheese
sour cream
avocado

Place chicken, water, and bouillon in medium saucepan. Sprinkle paprika over chicken. Cover and let simmer 30 minutes or until chicken falls away from the bone. Skin and bone chicken. Discard bones and skin. Cut chicken and return to pan. Add next six ingredients and simmer 30 minutes. Serve with chips, grated Monterey Jack cheese, sour cream, and avocados.

Chili Con Carne

1 cup small red beans
1 quart water
1/2 package chili seasoning

1/2 lb. hamburger
1/2 cup tomato sauce
1/2 cup mild salsa

Sort and wash beans. Pour water and beans into crock pot. Stir chili seasoning and 1/2 tsp. salt into beans. Cook 4 hours on high or 7 hours on low or until beans are tender. Brown hamburger with garlic powder, salt, and pepper. Drain fat and add meat to beans. Stir in salsa. Simmer another 10-15 minutes. Serve with chopped red onions and grated cheese on top.

Refried Beans

1 cup pinto beans
1 quart water
1 tsp. salt
1/2 tsp. garlic powder
1/4 tsp. chili powder

Sort and wash beans. Pour water and beans into crock pot. Stir salt and seasonings into beans. Cook 6-7 hours on high or until beans are tender. Mash beans by hand or puree in a blender. You may add 1/2 cup grated cheese when blending for creamier beans.
Serve with *Mexican rice, tortilla chips, and salsa.

Hamhocks-n-Beans

leftover ham bone (with meat) or
2 thick slices ham, cut into cubes
1 cup dry navy beans
1 quart water

1/4 cup chopped onions
1/2 tsp. salt
1/4 tsp. pepper
1/4 tsp. garlic powder

Put ham and 1 quart water in crock pot. Wash beans. Add beans, onions, and seasonings to crock pot. Stir well. Cook 6-7 hours on high or until beans are tender. Remove ham from bone. Discard bone and return ham to pot. Stir well and serve. Tastes delicious with homemade bread and butter.

Lentil Soup

2 slices bacon, cut up
1 cup dry lentils
1 quart water
1 cup canned diced tomatoes
1/4 cup chopped onions

1 carrot, peeled and chopped
1 Tbsp. parsley flakes
1 Tbsp. apple cider vinegar
1/4 tsp. garlic powder
1/2 tsp. Italian seasoning

Cook bacon pieces in crock pot. Add remaining ingredients and 1/2 tsp. salt to crock pot and stir well. Cook on high 2-3 hours or until lentils are tender. Serve with cornmeal muffins.

Love is Heaven... and Heaven is Love

Sir Walter Scott

My Favorite Recipes

_____
_____
_____
_____
_____
_____
_____
_____
_____
_____
_____
_____
_____
_____
_____
_____
_____
_____
_____
_____
_____
_____
_____
_____
_____

No Success can compensate for FAILURE in the HOME   David O. McKay

My Favorite Recipes

Casseroles and Quick Meals

Casseroles

Casseroles are simply the blending of a few different foods together to create a meal. There are some people who cringe when they hear the word "casserole," but I love casseroles. I think mixing different food flavors and textures gives an endless variety to our dinners. They are also nice for clean-up, as you don't have as many dishes to do. You don't want to overdo it, but I would suggest casseroles a couple of times a week.

Quick Meals

You won't always have a lot of time to prepare a nice dinner, so I have included many quick meal recipes in this section. I have also included some recipes for meals you can prepare ahead and freeze so you can quickly pop them in the oven or microwave.

Sloppy Joes

1/2 lb. hamburger
1/4 cup chopped onion
1/4 cup chopped celery
1/4 pkg. Sloppy Joe Seasoning

1 8-oz. can tomato sauce
3 Tbsp. ketchup
1/4 cup water
hamburger buns

Brown hamburger with salt, pepper, and garlic. Drain fat. Stir in remaining ingredients and simmer 30 minutes. Spread on hamburger buns. Serve with chopped fresh vegetables and dip. (Tip: This recipe can be made in a crock pot; add 1 tomato sauce can water, and cook 4-5 hours on low.)

Sloppy Joe Casserole

1 cup Sloppy Joe meat sauce
1 cup whole-kernel corn

2 cups Fritos corn chips
1/2 cup cheddar cheese

Mix all ingredients together in a casserole dish. Bake at 350 for 20 minutes.

Chili-Chip Casserole

1 cup chili con carne
1/4 cup salsa
1/4 cup sour cream
1/4 cup chopped olives

1/2 cup whole-kernel corn
1/2 cup grated cheese
20 corn tortilla chips

Mix all ingredients together in a casserole dish. Bake at 350 for 20 minutes.

Chicken Enchilada Casserole

1/2 cup shredded cooked chicken
1 small can diced green chilies
1/2 cup grated cheddar cheese

1/2 can cream of chicken soup
1/2 cup sour cream
4-5 yellow corn tortillas

Mix all ingredients except tortillas in small casserole dish. Tear tortillas into 2" pieces. Fold tortillas into mixture. Bake at 350 for 30 minutes. Serve with lettuce, sour cream, fresh-cut tomatoes, and salsa with an olive on top.

Chicken Enchiladas

1 cup shredded cooked chicken
1/2 cup grated cheddar cheese
1 small can enchilada sauce
4-5 yellow corn tortillas
shredded cheddar cheese

finely cut lettuce
sour cream
chopped avocado
salsa

Spread 1/2 enchilada sauce in small casserole dish. Mix chicken and 1/3 cup of grated cheese together. Spread chicken mixture down center of each tortilla. Roll tortillas and place in casserole dish. Top with remaining sauce and cheese. Bake at 350 for 30 minutes in oven or cook on high 6-7 minutes in microwave. Remove from oven. Serve with cheese, lettuce, sour cream, and salsa on top.

Quick-n-Easy Cheesy Enchiladas

4-6 yellow corn tortillas
1 small can enchilada sauce
1/2 cup grated cheddar cheese

finely cut lettuce
sour cream
black olives (opt.)

Spread cheese down center of tortillas. Roll tortillas and place in casserole dish. Pour enchilada sauce on top. Sprinkle with remaining cheese. Bake at 350 for 30 minutes or microwave on high 6-7 minutes. Serve on a bed of shredded lettuce and top with a dollop of sour cream and a black olive.

Beef Enchiladas

Brown and drain 1/2 lb. hamburger. Spread with cheese on tortillas. Cook as directed above.

Deluxe Enchiladas: Follow above recipe and top with sour cream, guacamole, chopped onions, peppers, tomatoes, olives, salsa, and shredded cheese.

We have been friends together,
In sunshine and in shade.

Caroline Elizabeth Sarah Norton

Tuna Rice Casserole

1 cup rice
1 can tuna
1/2 can cream of mushroom soup

1/2 can green beans
1/2 cup milk

Cook rice; stir remaining ingredients into rice. Serve with fresh fruit or salad.

Broccoli Ham Rice Bake

1/2 cup long-grain rice
1/2 cup chopped broccoli
1/3 cup chopped ham

1 1/4 cups boiling water
1 chicken bouillon cube
1/3 cup grated cheese

Spread first 3 ingredients in small casserole dish. Dissolve bouillon in boiling water. Pour boiling water over rice, broccoli, and ham and stir well. Sprinkle grated cheese over top. Bake at 350 for 30 minutes.

Egg-n-Rice Fajitas

1 box chicken-flavor Rice-a-Roni
4 eggs, well-beaten

4 or 5 flour tortillas
salsa

Cook Rice-a-Roni according to package directions. Cook and scramble eggs. Sprinkle with salt and pepper. Warm tortillas in microwave or in a skillet. Mix Rice-a-Roni and scrambled eggs and spread on tortilla. Top with salsa and roll up burrito-style.

Ham Fried Rice

2 cups cooked rice (better if one day old)   1/2 cup chopped ham

4 eggs, well-beaten   1/2 cup frozen peas

Heat 1 Tbsp. oil in frying skillet or wok. Add rice and stir-fry until slightly browned. Stir in eggs and continue stirring until eggs are cooked. Add ham and peas and heat through. You can serve this as a main dish with steamed broccoli or serve as a side dish with *Sweet and Sour Chicken.

Mexican Rice

4 slices bacon   1/2 cup rice

1 cup water   1/3 cup salsa

1/2 tsp. salt   1 tsp. chili powder

Cook and crumble bacon in medium saucepan. Remove bacon and pour water into bacon drippings. Bring water to a boil. Add remaining ingredients and stir well. Reduce heat, cover with lid, and simmer 20 minutes. Remove from heat and allow to sit 5 minutes before serving.

Spanish Rice: Substitute tomato sauce for salsa. Turn rice into casserole dish. Add 1/2 cup whole-kernel corn and sprinkle cheddar cheese on top. Bake at 350 for 10-15 minutes or until cheese is melted and bubbly.

75

Potato Chip Casserole

1 1/2 cups egg noodles
1 can water-packed tuna
1/4 cup milk

1/2 cup cream of celery soup
1/2 cup frozen peas
1 cup crushed potato chips

Cook egg noodles according to directions. Drain noodles. In a small casserole dish, combine tuna, milk, and soup and stir well. Fold in the noodles and peas. Sprinkle crushed potato chips on top. Bake at 400 for 20 minutes.

Ham and Broccoli Noodles

1 1/2 cups egg noodles
1/2 cup cubed ham
3/4 cup chopped broccoli
salt and pepper

1/2 cup cream of chicken soup
1/2 cup sour cream
1/2 cup mozzarella cheese
3 Tbsp. Parmesan cheese

Cook noodles according to package directions. Steam broccoli until tender. Drain noodles and broccoli. Spread noodles in bottom of casserole dish. Sprinkle with salt and pepper. Toss broccoli and ham over noodles. Mix sour cream and soup together and pour over top. Sprinkle with mozzarella and Parmesan cheese and bake at 400 for 20 minutes.

...by LOVE serve one another.

Galations 5:13

Quick Hamburger Gravy

Brown 1/2 lb. hamburger with salt, pepper, and garlic powder. Drain fat.

Add and stir well:

1/2 can cream of mushroom soup	1/2 cup sour cream
1 Tbsp. Worcestershire sauce	1/4 cup milk

Serve over baked potaoes, biscuits, or toast or mix with cooked rice.

Cheese Sauce

3 Tbsp. butter	1/4 tsp. salt
3 Tbsp. flour	1/3 cup grated cheese
1 cup milk	

Melt butter. Stir in flour to make smooth paste. Slowly stir in milk.
Cook and stir over medium heat until thickened and bubbly. Add cheese. Stir
until cheese is melted.

Baked Potato Bar

A potato bar is a great idea for a simple, inexpensive, yet very nutritious meal. Bake 2-4 potatoes at 425 for 45-60 minutes or until easy to pierce through with a fork. Slice potatoes lengthwise in half. Place two halves on plate open face. Serve with your choice of a variety of toppings. Some of my favorites include: butter, sour cream, green onions, shredded cheese, chili con carne, steamed broccoli, *quick hamburger gravy, and cheese sauce.

Easy Beef Stroganoff

1 1/2 cups egg noodles
1/2 lb. hamburger
1/4 cup chopped onion

1/2 can cream of mushroom soup
1/2 cup sour cream
2 tsp. Worcestershire sauce

Cook egg noodles according to package directions. Drain noodles. Meanwhile, brown hamburger with salt, pepper, and garlic powder. Add onions and cook a few more minutes. Drain fat. Stir in soup, sour cream, and Worcestershire sauce. Serve over noodles.

Tater Tot Casserole

1/2 lb. hamburger
1 1/2 cups Tater Tots

1/2 can cream of mushroom soup
1 cup French-sliced green beans

Brown hamburger with salt, pepper, and garlic powder. Drain fat and spread meat in small casserole dish. Layer green beans on meat. Spoon soup evenly over green beans. Spread Tater Tots on top. Bake at 400 for 20-25 minutes.

Hash Brown Casserole

Follow recipe for Tater Tot Casserole, substituting 1 cup frozen peas for the green beans and 1 1/2 cups hash browns for the Tater Tots. (Note: chop leftover baked potatoes to make hash browns.)

Yummy Potatoes

3 whole, unpeeled potatoes
1/4 cup chopped onions
2 Tbsp. butter
1/2 can cream of chicken soup

1/2 cup sour cream
1/2 cup grated cheese
2 Tbsp. butter
1 cup crushed corn flakes

Boil unpeeled potatoes 15-20 minutes or until tender, but firm. Remove from heat. Run under cold water. Allow to cool. Meanwhile, sauté onions in 2 Tbsp. butter until they start to turn brown. Mix onions with soup, sour cream, and cheese in casserole dish and stir well. Peel and cut potatoes into small pieces. Stir potatoes into sauce. Sauté corn flakes in remaining 2 Tbsp. butter. Sprinkle corn flakes over top of potatoes. Bake at 350 for 30 minutes.

Creamy Sour Potatoes

3 medium potatoes, boiled and cubed
1/4 cup chopped green onion
3 Tbsp. butter
1/2 cup sour cream
1 Tbsp. apple cider vinegar
1/2 cup grated cheddar cheese

Sauté green onions in butter. Add sour cream and vinegar and stir well. Turn into a casserole dish. Stir in potatoes and cheese. Bake at 350 for 30 minutes.

Bacon and Cheese Potatoes: Add 1/4 cup bacon bits to above recipe.

Zucchini Casserole

1 cup chopped zucchini
1/4 cup chopped onion
1/4 cup grated carrots
1/3 cup cream of chicken soup

1/3 cup cheddar cheese
1/3 cup sour cream
1 box chicken stuffing mix

Steam zucchini, onions, and carrots 5-10 minutes or until zucchini is just tender but still firm. In a small casserole dish, combine soup, cheese, and sour cream. Drain vegetables. You can use water from vegetables to make stuffing. Prepare stuffing according to package directions. Stir vegetables into sauce. Spread the stuffing on top. Bake at 350 for 30 minutes.

Stuffed Ham Rolls

1 box chicken stuffing mix
2 Tbsp. butter

1 4-oz. package cream cheese
4 slices ham

Make stuffing according to package. Spread cream cheese on ham slices to 1/2" from edge. Place 1/3 cup stuffing down center of ham. Roll up ham slices and secure with toothpicks. Bake at 350 for 15-20 minutes.

Pigs in Blankets

2 hot dogs cut in half, and in half again lengthwise
8 refrigerator biscuits

Press biscuits into the size of small pizzas. Place hot dog on biscuit and roll up. Bake at 400 for for 10 minutes. Serve with ketchup and mustard.

Pizza Wheels

8-10 refrigerator biscuits
1 cup spaghetti sauce

1/2 c. mozzarella cheese
choice of toppings

Press biscuits into small pizza crusts. Spread sauce on top. Sprinkle with cheese and choice of toppings. Bake at 400 for 10-12 minutes.

Chicken Dumplings

1/2 cup cooked chopped chicken
1 green onion, chopped
1 rib celery, chopped

3/4 cup cream of chicken soup
3/4 cup milk
1 package refrigerator biscuits

Mix chopped chicken, onion, and celery together. Press biscuits into shape of small pizzas. Place 2 Tbsp. of chicken mix in center of biscuit. Fold edges to center and pinch dough together. Mix soup and milk in skillet. Place biscuits in gravy, cover, and cook over medium-low heat for 15-20 minutes.

Baked Beans

2 strips of bacon
1 can pork and beans
1/4 cup chopped onion
1/4 cup chopped green pepper

3 Tbsp. tomato ketchup
1 1/2 Tbsp. mustard
1/4 cup brown sugar
1 tsp. Worcestershire sauce

Cook and crumble bacon. Reserve bacon drippings. Drain pork and beans. Mix drippings and all ingredients in a small casserole dish. Cover and bake at 350 for 20 minutes. Uncover and bake 10 more minutes.

Beans and Franks

Follow recipe for baked beans, but substitute 2-3 franks for the bacon and omit the green peppers. Slice franks and fry in skillet on both sides of slices. Combine all ingredients and bake as above.

Fried Franks and Macaroni

2-3 franks (hot dogs)   1 box macaroni and cheese

Make macaroni and cheese as directed. Slice franks into 1/4" circles. Fry on both sides in skillet. Stir into prepared macaroni and cheese. Serve with red applesauce. (Make red applesauce by mixing 3 Tbsp. strawberry Jello mix with 1 cup applesauce.)

My Favorite Recipes

_____
_____
_____
_____
_____
_____
_____
_____
_____
_____
_____
_____
_____
_____
_____
_____
_____
_____
_____
_____
_____
_____
_____
_____

No Success can compensate for FAILURE in the HOME   David O. McKay

My Favorite Recipes

A Menu for Two

Dinner for Two

This section is filled with dinner recipes for your special occasions. They either take more time to prepare or the ingredients cost a little more than some of the other recipes in this book. But if your budget will allow it and you have enough time, the recipes in this section are perfect for a...

dinner for two!

The recipes in this section are for the main dish only, but there are suggested side dishes that go with each main dish. The recipes for the side dishes are found in other sections of this book.

Spaghetti Sauce

1 lb. hamburger
1 16-oz. can crushed tomatoes
2 8-oz. cans tomato sauce

2 Tbsp. Italian seasoning
2 Tbsp. sugar
1 garlic clove

Brown hamburger with salt, pepper, and garlic powder in a medium sauce-pan. Drain fat. Stir in tomatoes, sauce, seasoning, and sugar. Press garlic with garlic press or use 1 tsp. minced garlic. Add garlic to sauce and stir well. Simmer 1 hour or until sauce thickens and turns deep red in color. Serve over cooked spaghetti noodles. Sprinkle with Parmesan cheese.

Tip: Do not rinse noodles, as this rinses off the starch. The starch makes the noodles sticky, which helps the sauce stick to the noodles.

Spaghetti and Meatballs

Follow recipe for meatballs (page 92), but don't pour barbecue sauce in casserole dish. Bake 20-25 minutes or until done. Place meatballs on top of noodles and pour spaghetti sauce from above recipe over noodles and meatballs. You can also cook meatballs on your stove top. Place meatballs in skillet, cover, and cook on medium-low heat 15-20 minutes, turning often.

Meaty Baked Lasagna

1 lb. hambuger
4 lasagna noodles
1 cup spaghetti sauce
3/4 cup mozzarella cheese

2/3 cup sour cream or
    cottage cheese
6 Tbsp. Parmesan cheese
3 tsp. parsley flakes

Brown hamburger with salt, pepper, and garlic powder. Drain fat. Boil water and cook noodles according to package directions, making sure not to over-cook the pasta. Drain and cut lasagna to fit length of 8x8" casserole dish. Use leftover noodles for top layer. Spread 1/4 cup sauce in bottom of dish.

Make two layers of the following:

2 noodles, 1/3 cup sour cream or cottage cheese, 1/2 of the browned meat, 1/4 cup sauce, 2 Tbsp. Parmesan cheese, and 1 tsp. parsley.

Top with remaining noodles, sauce, mozzarella, and Parmesan cheese. Bake at 350 for 30-40 minutes or until cheese is melted and bubbly. Serve with French bread or garlic toast and green salad.

Spinach Lasagna

Thaw and drain 2/3 cup frozen chopped spinach. Follow directions for baked lasagna, substituting spinach for the browned meat.

Fettuccine Alfredo

1 cup fettuccine pasta
2 Tbsp. butter
2 Tbsp. flour
1 cup milk

1/4 tsp. garlic powder
1/4 tsp. salt
2 Tbsp. Parmesan cheese
parsley flakes

Cook fettuccine according to directions. Melt butter. Stir flour into butter until you have a nice paste. Slowly stir in milk. Cook and stir over medium heat until thickened and bubbly. Stir in garlic and salt and cook one more minute. Remove from heat and stir in Parmesan cheese. Divide pasta onto two plates. Pour Alfredo sauce over pasta and sprinkle parsley on top.

Chicken Fettuccine

Follow above directions, but add 1/2 cup chopped cooked chicken to sauce in place of the Parmesan cheese. Warm through. Serve with Italian herb bread and green salad.

Italian Herb Bread

2-4 slices French bread
1/4 cup butter (softened)

1/4 tsp. garlic salt
1 tsp. Italian seasoning

Mix butter, garlic salt, and Italian seasoning together. Spread over bread. Broil until golden brown on edges.

89

Ritzy Chicken

2 boneless skinless chicken breasts
1/2 cup plain yogurt or sour cream
10 Ritz crackers
1/4 cup Parmesan cheese
1 tsp. garlic powder

1 Tbsp. parsley flakes
1/4 tsp. pepper
1/2 tsp. salt
1/2 can cream of chicken soup
1/2 cup canned milk

Crush the crackers to make coarse crumbs. Mix crumbs with Parmesan cheese, garlic powder, parsley, salt, and pepper. Pour mixture in zip-top bag or shallow dish. Dip chicken into yogurt and then in crumb mixture to coat chicken. Place chicken in baking pan. Bake at 425 for 50-60 minutes or until chicken is crisp and golden brown. Mix soup and milk. Heat through and pour over chicken.

For a very nice dinner, you could serve chicken with Heavenly Dinner Rolls and Sautéed Vegetables.

Ritzy Pork Chops

Follow above recipe, substituting pork chops for the chicken breasts. For the gravy, use cream of celery or cream of mushroom soup in place of the cream of chicken soup.

Serve with biscuits and cooked green beans for a real country-tasting meal.

Chicken Chimichangas

3-4 flour tortillas
Filling: 1 cup shredded cooked chicken
       1/2 cup cream of chicken soup
       1/4 cup finely diced onion

1 cup vegetable oil for cooking chimichangas in a heavy skillet or Dutch oven

Choice of toppings:
       Finely cut lettuce, chopped tomatoes, peppers, onions, black olives,
         sour cream, guacamole, shredded cheddar cheese, and fresh salsa

Heat oil. Mix together the chicken, soup, and onion. Spread chicken mixture down center of each tortilla. Fold sides over and roll up burrito-style. Put a match in oil. When the oil is hot enough, the match will light. Remove match from oil. Using tongs, place chimichanga in hot oil. Turn quickly to cook both sides until golden. Place on paper towels to drain excess oil. Serve with your choice of toppings. These taste great with refried beans and Mexican rice.

Cooked chicken: Place 2 chicken breasts in pan with 1" water. Sprinkle paprika and chicken bouillon over chicken. Steam 20-30 minutes. Shred in pan while chicken absorbs the juices.

Beef Chimichangas

Follow the same directions for the chicken chimichangas, but replace the chicken with shredded roast beef and the soup with canned refried beans.

Mom's Meatloaf

1 lb. hamburger
1 egg
10 saltine crackers
1 8-oz. can tomato sauce
1/4 cup chopped onion

1/4 cup chopped green pepper
1/2 tsp. salt
1/2 tsp. garlic powder
1 tsp. Italian seasoning
   ketchup

Mix all ingredients thoroughly and place in casserole dish. Bake at 350 for 45 minutes. Spread ketchup over top and bake additional 15 minutes at 400.

Bake a few potatoes along with your meatloaf. They take about the same time to cook. Steam carrots and broccoli, and you have a meal.

Meatballs

Follow meatloaf recipe, but form the mixture into balls. Place in casserole dish. Pour barbecue sauce over top. Bake 1 hour at 350.

Perfect Pot Roast:

3- to 4-lb. pot roast   1 tsp. beef bouillon

Rub bouillon on roast. Place roast in crock pot. Cover and cook on high for 3-4 hours or on low 5-6 hours. Turn off crock pot and baste with juices. Allow meat to cool 15 to 20 minutes before slicing. Use remaining drippings to make gravy.

Brown Gravy:

1/2 cup drippings   1/4 cup flour
1/4 tsp. beef bouillon   1 1/2 cups water

Blend flour and drippings together. Pour into saucepan and slowly stir in water. Add bouillon. Cook and stir over medium heat until gravy comes to a full boil. Continue cooking and stirring until thickened and bubbly. Serve over mashed potatoes.

Mashed Potatoes:

3-4 medium potatoes   3 Tbsp. butter
1 tsp. salt   1/4 cup milk

Peel and chop potatoes. Place potatoes in pot with water to cover potatoes. Sprinkle with salt. Cook over medium heat 30-40 minutes or until potatoes are tender. Remove from heat and drain water. Put potatoes in bowl and mash. Add butter and milk and whip with hand mixer.

Baked Ham with Pineapple

4 thick slices ham
4 pineapple rings

1/3 cup brown sugar
pineapple juice

Place pineapple rings evenly in a casserole dish. Sprinkle with brown sugar and pineapple juice. Lay ham slices on top and bake at 350 for 30 minutes.

Dinner in a Pumpkin

Cut the top off a small pumpkin as you would to make a jack-o-lantern. Clean out pumpkin. Brown 1/2 lb. hamburger with salt, pepper, and garlic powder. Drain fat. Add 1 cup cooked rice, 1/4 cup chopped onions, 1/2 cup cream of mushroom soup, and 1/4 cup milk. Stir together and pour into pumpkin. Replace pumpkin lid and place pumpkin in oven on a baking sheet, and bake at 375 for 1-2 hours. Place pumpkin on on serving platter, Serve dinner out of the pumpkin.

Cranberry Pork Chops

2 Tbsp. vegetable oil
2 Tbsp. apple cider vinegar
2 Tbsp. honey

1 tsp. poultry seasoning
3/4 cup cranberry sauce
2-4 pork chops

Mix first five ingredients together. Place pork chops in casserole dish. Pour sauce over pork chops. Cover with foil and bake at 375 for 45 minutes. Remove foil and bake an additional 15 minutes.
Serve with rice or egg noodles.

Apricot Chicken

2 medium chicken breasts
1/2 cup apricot jam
3 Tbsp. lemon juice

1/4 tsp. nutmeg
salt and pepper

Place chicken breasts in small casserole dish. Mix apricot jam, lemon juice, and nutmeg. Sprinkle chicken with salt and pepper. Spread apricot sauce over chicken. Cover with foil. Bake at 375 for 45 minutes. Remove foil and bake an additional 15 minutes. Serve with wild rice.

... to love and be loved is the greatest happiness of existence.

Sydney Smith

Chunky Chicken Gravy

1 large chicken breast
1 chicken bouillon cube
paprika

3 Tbsp. butter
3 Tbsp. flour
2 cups milk

Place 1" water in saucepan. Dissolve bouillon in water. Place chicken in water and sprinkle paprika, salt, and pepper over chicken. Cover and let simmer on medium-low heat for 30-40 minutes or until chicken is tender. Remove pan from heat. Leaving chicken in the water, cut chicken into small pieces. Sprinkle flour over chicken and stir well. Add butter and milk. Cook and stir over medium heat until butter melts. Continue stirring and cooking until gravy boils and thickens. Remove from heat. Serve over mashed potatoes, biscuits, or toast.

Hawaiian Haystacks

1 1/2 cups cooked rice
1 cup chunky chicken gravy
1/2 cup chow mein noodles

Cook rice according to directions. Place a scoop of rice on plate and pour gravy on top. Sprinkle with chow mein noodles and choice of toppings:
shredded cheese, chopped onions, peppers, celery, tomatoes, olives, peas, pineapple chunks, nuts, mandarin oranges, and coconut.

Marinated and Grilled Chicken

1 lb. boneless skinless chicken breasts   1/2 cup soy sauce
1 cup 7-Up or other lemon-lime soda   1/4 tsp. garlic powder
1/2 cup vegetable oil

Cut chicken into 2" strips. Combine remaining ingredients in a bowl. Place the chicken in bowl and make sure chicken is covered with marinade. Cover tightly and place in refrigerator. Shake bowl occasionally. To grill chicken: Place on grill and cook several minutes on each side until chicken looks done. If you don't have a grill, you can broil chicken in your oven by placing broiling pan on bottom rack of oven.

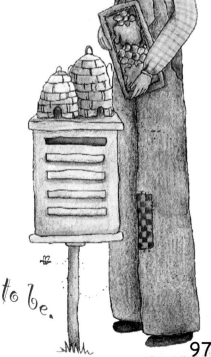

Chicken Ham Rolls

2 thick slices ham   1/4 cup barbecue sauce
2 slices cheese (any kind) 2/3 cup cooked chicken

Spread barbecue sauce on ham slices. Place cheese on sauce and spread shredded cooked chicken down center of cheese. Wrap ham slices around chicken and secure with toothpicks. Bake at 350 for 20-25 minutes.

Grow old along with me... the best is yet to be.

Robert Browning

97

Barbecued Beef Sandwiches

1 small beef roast
1 cup barbecue sauce
1 tsp. Worcestershire sauce

1/3 cup chopped onion
2 Tbsp. honey
2 Tbsp. mustard

Dissolve bouillon in 1/4 cup water. Place roast in crock pot and rub bouillon into roast. Cook on high for 2 hours. Pour barbecue sauce and Worcestershire sauce over roast. Sprinkle onions over sauce. Pour honey and mustard over onions. Reduce heat to low and cook 3-4 hours. Shred meat and stir. Serve on hoagie rolls with Dutch oven potatoes.

Dutch Oven Potatoes

You can make Dutch oven potatoes using your crock pot. They are easy to prepare and you can let them cook all day. Place the following in a crock pot:

4 slices bacon, chopped
4 potatoes, peeled and thinly sliced
salt and pepper
1/3 cup onions, thinly sliced
1 can cream of mushroom soup
1 4-oz. can diced green chilies (opt.)

Cook on low 5-6 hours or high 3-4 hours. Check and stir occasionally.

Oven-Baked Pizza

Pizza Crust: 1 cup warm water   3 cups flour
             1 1/2 tsp. active dry yeast   1/2 tsp. salt
             2 tsp. sugar   3 Tbsp. vegetable oil

Dissolve yeast in water. Using a mixer, blend in 2 cups of flour and remaining ingredients. Mix until well-blended. Stir in remaining flour. Knead on floured surface 3-4 minutes. Cover and let rest 30 minutes. Punch dough down and shape into a ball. Roll out ball or stretch by hand to fit a 12" greased pizza pan. (Note: For a crisp crust, sprinkle a little cornmeal on pan.)

Pizza Sauce: 1 8-oz. can tomato sauce   1/2 tsp. garlic powder
             1 Tbsp. sugar   1 tsp. Italian seasoning

Combine all ingredients in a saucepan. Simmer 3-5 minutes or until sauce starts to deepen in color. Spread over pizza crust and layer with grated mozzarella cheese and desired toppings. Bake at 450 for 15-20 minutes.

Chicken Garlic Pizza: Follow above directions, but make Alfredo Sauce from the dinner section. Spread sauce over crust. Sprinkle with garlic salt. Spread chunks of cooked chicken over pizza and top with Parmesan and mozzarella cheeses.

My Favorite Recipes

Fruits and Veggies

5 a day for better health...that's what the guidelines say.

This section will help you meet the daily requirements for fruits and vegetables. It is packed with recipes for fresh garden produce or canned fruits and vegetables and some tips for choosing good produce.

*For thou shalt eat the
labour of thine hands
happy shalt thou be,
and it shall be
well with thee.*

Psalms 128:2

Creamy Cucumbers

1 cucumber, finely sliced
2 Tbsp. onion, finely chopped
1/4 cup sour cream

2 tsp. vinegar
1 tsp. sugar
1/4 tsp. salt

Mix the sliced cucumbers with the onions. Combine remaining ingredients for dressing. Mix dressing with vegetables. Cover and refrigerate until ready to serve

Carrot-Raisin Salad

1 cup grated carrots   3 Tbsp. salad dressing   1/4 cup raisins

Peel and grate enough carrots to make 1 cup. Mix in salad dressing and raisins. Cover and refrigerate until ready to serve.

Stuffed Tomatoes

2 tomatoes   1/2 cup cottage cheese   seasoning salt

Slice tomatoes as you would a pizza into wedges, cutting down just short of the bottom. Let slices fall out to open tomato. Stuff 1/4 cup cottage cheese in each tomato. Sprinkle with seasoning salt or paprika.

Take time to enjoy the fruits of your labors !

Wilted Spinach Salad

1 1/2 cups torn spinach leaves
2 Tbsp. chopped red onion
2 slices bacon
1 hard-boiled egg, chopped

2 tsp. vinegar
1 tsp. lemon juice
1/2 tsp. sugar
1/4 tsp. salt

Toss spinach and onion in a bowl. Cook and crumble bacon. Do not drain fat. Stir in remaining ingredients. Remove from heat. Add spinach and onion. Toss until well coated. Divide salad on two plates and top with chopped egg. Serve immediately. This salad is great with spaghetti or lasagna.

Creamy Romaine Salad

1 1/2 cups torn romaine lettuce leaves
2 slices bacon, cooked and crumbled
1/4 cup grated mozzarella cheese
1/4 cup cottage cheese
2 Tbsp. chopped red onion

1/4 cup vegetable oil
1 1/2 Tbsp. vinegar
3 Tbsp. sugar
1/2 tsp. poppy seeds
1/4 tsp. salt

Combine last five ingredients for dressing. Allow to marinate for a few hours. Toss first four ingredients in a bowl. Stir dressing and pour over salad. Mix well. Serve immediately. Tastes great with ham or chicken.

Cranberry Poppy Seed Salad

1 1/2 cups torn salad greens
1/3 cup dried cranberries

1/3 cup grated Swiss cheese
poppy seed dressing

Make poppy seed dressing from Creamy Romaine salad recipe. Allow dressing to sit for a few hours. Place greens in two salad bowls. Sprinkle cheese and dried cranberries on top. Pour dressing over salad and serve immediately.

☆Orange Spinach Toss

1 1/2 cups torn spinach leaves
1 4-oz. can mandarin oranges
1/4 cup water chestnuts
1/4 cup slivered almonds
1 tsp. sesame seeds

2 Tbsp. vegetable oil
1 Tbsp. lemon juice
1/2 tsp. poppy seeds
1 Tbsp. sugar
1/4 tsp. salt

Toss spinach leaves with mandarin oranges and water chestnuts. Sauté almonds and sesame seeds in 1 Tbsp. butter for 2-3 minutes. Blend together last five ingredients. Place salad in two bowls. Sprinkle almonds and sesame seeds over salad. Shake or stir dressing again and pour over salad. Serve immediately.

Sauteed Vegetables

1 Tbsp. vegetable oil
3 small red potatoes
8 peeled baby carrots
1/2 cup chopped broccoli

1/2 cup chopped cauliflower
1/2 tsp. Italian seasoning
1 Tbsp. butter
salt and pepper

Place carrots and potatoes in 1 cup of water in a saucepan. Cover and steam on medium-low for 15 minutes. Add broccoli and cauliflower and steam 5 more minutes. Drain water. Heat oil in skillet. Turn vegetables into hot oil. Sprinkle with salt and pepper and stir-fry several minutes until vegetables are tender. Stir in butter and Italian seasoning until butter melts. Serve with Ritzy Chicken.

Cooked Carrots

2-3 carrots, peeled and sliced
1/2 cup water

salt and pepper
1 tsp. butter (opt.)

Place carrots and water in a small saucepan. Sprinkle with salt and pepper. Cover with tight-fitting lid and cook at medium-low for 20 minutes or until carrots are tender. Drain and serve with butter if desired.

Broccoli and Cheese Sauce

2 cups chopped broccoli	1 Tbsp. flour
1/2 cup water	1 cup milk
1/4 tsp. salt	1/2 tsp. salt
1 Tbsp. butter	1 cup grated cheese

Place chopped broccoli and water in saucepan. Sprinkle with 1/4 tsp. salt. Cover with tight-fitting lid and cook on medium-low for 10-15 minutes or until broccoli is tender.

Cheese Sauce: Melt butter in saucepan. Stir in flour. Slowly stir in milk to avoid lumps. Add the 1/2 tsp. salt and cook and stir over medium heat. Bring to a boil. Continue to cook and stir until sauce is thickened. Add grated cheddar cheese and stir until cheese is melted. Serve over steamed broccoli.

Spicy Cheese Sauce: Follow above directions and add 1 4-oz. can diced jalapeno or chili peppers with the grated cheese. Serve over baked potatoes or tortilla chips.

Creamed Peas

1 cup frozen peas
1 Tbsp. butter
1 Tbsp. flour

2/3 cup milk
1/4 tsp. salt
dash of pepper

Thaw frozen peas. Meanwhile, melt butter in a saucepan. Stir in flour until well mixed. Slowly add milk while stirring to avoid lumps. Add 1/2 tsp. salt and a dash of pepper. Cook and stir over medium heat. Bring to a boil and continue cooking and stirring until sauce thickens. Stir in thawed peas and warm through. Serve with roast beef or meatloaf.

Parmesan Creamed Peas: Stir in 1 Tbsp. Parmesan cheese to above recipe.

Slivered Almond Green Beans

1/2 can green beans, undrained
2 Tbsp. slivered almonds

1 Tbsp. butter
1/2 tsp. lemon juice

Cook green beans in liquid according to label directions. Drain hot green beans. In a skillet, melt butter and sauté almonds for 3-5 minutes or until golden. Remove from heat. Stir in lemon juice and drained green beans.

Almond-Mushroom Green Beans: Follow above directions and sauté 1/4 cup sliced mushrooms and 1/4 cup sliced onions with almonds. Add 1/4 tsp. garlic to melted butter. Replace the lemon juice with 1 tsp. soy sauce. Serve with chicken, beef, or pork chops.

Green Bean Bake

1/2 can French-sliced green beans
1/2 can cream of mushroom soup
1/2 cup milk

1/2 tsp. seasoning salt
1/2 cup canned
French-fried onions

Drain beans and spread in bottom of a small casserole dish. Mix soup and milk together and pour over green beans. Sprinkle with seasoning salt and top with French-fried onions. Bake at 350 for 20 minutes.

Zucchini Marinara

1 1/2 cups sliced zucchini
1 Tbsp. butter
salt and pepper
1/2 cup spaghetti noodles

1 8-oz. can tomato sauce
2 Tbsp. sugar
1/2 tsp. garlic powder
1 tsp. Italian seasoning

Cook spaghetti noodles according to package directions. Cook sliced zucchini in 1/2 cup water over medium-low heat until tender. Drain squash and stir in the butter, then sprinkle with salt and pepper. In a saucepan, mix together tomato sauce, sugar, garlic powder, and Italian seasoning. Simmer 3-5 minutes. Divide noodles onto two plates. Layer zucchini on noodles and pour marinara sauce over zucchini and noodles. Sprinkle with Parmesan cheese if desired. Serve with French bread and butter or toasted garlic bread.

Raspberry Pretzel Salad

1 cup small pretzels
1 cup frozen raspberries
1 4-oz. package cream cheese
1/4 cup powdered sugar

1 tsp. vanilla
1 3-oz. package raspberry Jell-O
1 cup boiling water
1/2 cup crushed pineapple

Break pretzels and spread at bottom of small casserole dish. Sprinkle frozen raspberries and drained pineapple on top. Dissolve Jell-O in boiling water. Pour Jell-O over fruit. Refrigerate 3-4 hours or until set. Blend cream cheese, sugar, and vanilla together. Spread over Jell-O. Refrigerate until ready to serve.

Fruit Cocktail Salad

1 3-oz. package strawberry Jello
1 cup boiling water

1/2 cup cottage cheese
1 cup fruit cocktail

Dissolve Jello in boiling water. Spread cottage cheese in the bottom of a small casserole dish. Drain fruit cocktail and spread over cottage cheese. Pour Jello over fruit cocktail. Refrigerate 3-4 hours or until set.

Peach Jello Salad: Blend 1 4-oz. package softened cream cheese with 1/4 cup powdered sugar and 1 tsp. vanilla. Spread on bottom of small casserole dish. Spread 1 cup drained canned peaches over cream cheese. Dissolve 1 3-oz. package of peach Jello in 1 cup boiling water. Pour over peaches. Refrigerate 3-4 hours or until set.

Creamy Jell-O Salad

1 4-oz. package cream cheese
1/2 small package Jell-O (any flavor)

1/2 cup canned fruit with juice
(any flavor--I like pineapple)

Boil 1/2 cup water in saucepan. Dissolve Jell-O in water. Combine Jell-O, fruit, and cream cheese in blender. Mix until smooth. Pour into casserole dish. Refrigerate until firm (2-3 hours).

Strawberry-Banana Salad

1 cup fresh strawberries
2 bananas
1 can mandarin oranges
1/4 cup coconut (opt.)

1/2 package strawberry Jell-O
1/2 cup whipping cream
3 Tbsp. powdered sugar
1/2 tsp. vanilla

Wash, hull, and slice strawberries. Sprinkle 2 Tbsp. sugar over strawberries and allow to sit. Slice bananas and drain oranges. Mix cream with powdered sugar. Whip cream with electric mixer until soft peaks form. Add vanilla and Jell-O. Beat for one more minute. Stir fruit and coconut into whipped cream. Chill in freezer 20-30 minutes just before serving.

You catch more flies...
with honey!

Denny K. Harman

111

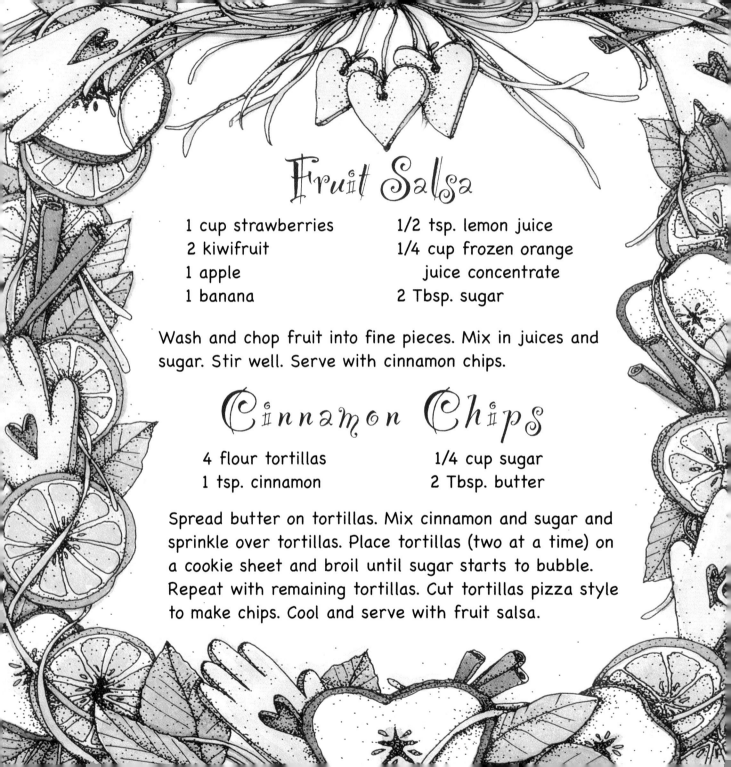

Fruit Salsa

1 cup strawberries
2 kiwifruit
1 apple
1 banana

1/2 tsp. lemon juice
1/4 cup frozen orange
     juice concentrate
2 Tbsp. sugar

Wash and chop fruit into fine pieces. Mix in juices and sugar. Stir well. Serve with cinnamon chips.

Cinnamon Chips

4 flour tortillas
1 tsp. cinnamon

1/4 cup sugar
2 Tbsp. butter

Spread butter on tortillas. Mix cinnamon and sugar and sprinkle over tortillas. Place tortillas (two at a time) on a cookie sheet and broil until sugar starts to bubble. Repeat with remaining tortillas. Cut tortillas pizza style to make chips. Cool and serve with fruit salsa.

Fresh Berry Fruit Dip

1 cup fresh berries

3 Tbsp. sugar

2 Tbsp. frozen orange
   juice concentrate

1/4 cup powdered sugar

1 6-oz. vanilla yogurt

1/8 tsp. nutmeg

Wash and gently mash berries. Mix with sugar and orange juice. Mix powdered sugar, yogurt, and nutmeg together. Blend in fruit. Serve with cinnamon chips, pretzels, or vanilla wafers.

Sweet Lemon Fruit Dip

1 6-oz. vanilla yogurt

1/4 cup cream cheese

1 Tbsp. lemon juice

1 tsp. grated lemon peel

3 Tbsp. powdered sugar

Mix cream cheese until soft. Blend with remaining ingredients. Serve with fresh-cut apples and orange slices.

Vanilla Fruit Dip: Prepare as above, but substitute 1 tsp. vanilla for the grated lemon and lemon juice. Serve with fresh-cut melons, grapes, strawberries, and pineapple.

Fruit Smoothie

1 cup milk

1/4 cup sugar

1 tsp. vanilla

1 cup frozen fruit

You can buy frozen fruit or freeze your own. Apricots, strawberries, and bananas work great for this recipe. Wash fruit and place in zip-top bags. Pit apricots before freezing. For bananas, keep in skins to freeze.

In a blender, pour milk, sugar, and vanilla. Add frozen fruit a few pieces at a time and blend on high. Continue adding fruit and blending until thick.

Fruit Slush

1 cup fruit (any kind)

1 cup ice cubes

1/4 cup sugar

1 tsp. vanilla

Pour all ingredients in blender and blend on high until ice cubes turn to slush.

☆Old-Fashioned Lemonade

2 lemons

1/2 cup sugar

1 tsp. corn syrup

1 quart water

Stir sugar and corn syrup into water until sugar dissolves. Squeeze lemons into sugar water. Stir well. Pour into glasses filled with ice cubes.

My Favorite Recipes

No Success can compensate for FAILURE in the HOME   David O. McKay

My Favorite Recipes

Desserts and Snacks

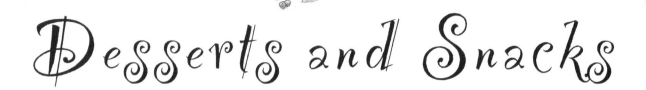

Desserts and Snacks

Whether you like cherry cheesecake or chocolate brownies for dessert or a late-night snack, you will LOVE this section! It's packed with treats to satisfy every sweet tooth.

Our Hearts are pulled together through the friendship that we share!

And if you are in the mood for something a bit salty, there are also recipes for some savory snacks in this section.

Peach Cobbler

2 cups sliced peaches	1/3 cup water	1/4 tsp. salt
1/4 cup brown sugar	1/2 cup flour	3 Tbsp. butter
1 Tbsp. cornstarch	3/4 tsp. baking powder	1 egg
1/4 tsp. nutmeg	2 Tbsp. sugar	2 Tbsp. milk

Spread peaches in a small casserole dish. Sprinkle 2 tsp. lemon juice on top. In a saucepan, combine the next four ingredients. Cook and stir over medium heat until thickened and bubbly. Pour over peaches. Sift dry ingredients together. Cut in butter until mix is crumbly. Stir together milk and egg. Add all at once to dry mix and stir just until moist. Drop evenly over peaches. Bake at 400 for 20 minutes. Serve warm with a scoop of vanilla ice cream on top of each piece.

Strawberries-n-Cream Cake

1 1/3 cups flour	1/3 cup 2% milk	strawberry punch
1 1/4 tsp. baking powder	1 egg, slightly-beaten	1/2 cup sugar
1/4 cup butter	1 tsp. vanilla	1 Tbsp. cornstarch
3/4 cup sugar	yellow food coloring	1/2 cup water

Sift dry ingredients together. Add milk and eggs and beat with electric mixer 2-3 minutes. Add vanilla and food coloring and beat 2 more minutes. Pour into greased cake pan and bake at 375 for 30-35 minutes. Cool completely. Spread strawberry topping evenly over cake. Spread whipping cream on top.

Strawberry Topping: In a saucepan, blend strawberry punch, sugar, cornstarch, and water. Cook and stir until thickened. Stir in 3/4 cup sliced strawberries.

Dreamy Chocolate Cream Pies

2 single-size graham cracker crusts
1 small package cook-and-serve
   chocolate pudding

1 1/2 cups whole milk
caramel topping
whipping cream

Make pudding according to package directions, using only 1 1/2 cups whole milk. Let cool five minutes. Stir pudding and pour into prepared crusts. Place plastic wrap on pudding to prevent skin from forming. Refrigerate. Just before serving, drizzle caramel topping over pudding and top with whipped cream.

Whipped cream: With a mixer, beat 1 cup whipping cream, 1/2 tsp. vanilla, and 1/4 cup powdered sugar until cream forms into soft peaks.

Banana Cream Pies

2 single-size graham cracker crusts
1 medium banana
1 small package cook-and-serve
   vanilla pudding
1 1/2 cups whole milk

Make pudding according to package directions, using only 1 1/2 cups whole milk. Let cool five minutes. Meanwhile, peel and slice banana. Place banana slices on bottom of pie shells. Pour pudding over bananas. Put plastic wrap on pudding to prevent skin from forming. Refrigerate. Just before serving, spread some whipped cream on each pie if desired.

Carrot-Raisin Cake

1/4 cup oil
1/2 cup sugar
1 egg
1 cup flour
1/2 tsp. baking soda
1/4 tsp. cinnamon

1/2 cup finely grated carrots
1/4 cup chopped walnuts (opt.)
1/4 tsp. salt
1/2 tsp. vanilla
1/4 cup raisins (opt.)
1/2 cup crushed pineapple

Mix oil, sugar, and egg together. Sift dry ingredients together and add to oil mixture. Stir in remaining ingredients and pour into greased 8x8 baking pan. Bake at 350 for 30-40 minutes. Cool and frost with cream cheese icing.

Cream Cheese Icing: Beat 1/4 cup cream cheese, 2 Tbsp. butter, and 1 cup powdered sugar until creamy.

Pineapple Upside-Down Cake

1/4 cup oil
1/2 cup sugar
1 egg

1 cup flour
1/2 tsp. baking powder
1/4 tsp. salt

1/2 tsp. cinnamon
1/4 tsp. nutmeg

Mix oil, sugar, and egg together. Sift dry ingredients into oil mixture. In an 8x8 baking pan, spread 1 cup crushed pineapple. Sprinkle 1/2 cup brown sugar over pineapple. Pour batter over pineapple and bake at 350 for 30 minutes. Turn upside down to serve. Top with a dollop of whipped cream.

Caramel Apple Cake

3 medium apples	1 tsp. baking soda
3/4 cup sugar	1/2 tsp. salt
1/3 cup butter	1/2 tsp. cinnamon
1 egg	1/4 tsp. cloves
1 cup flour	1/3 cup chopped walnuts

Wash, core, and grate apples. Cream butter, sugar, and egg together. Stir in grated apples. Sift dry ingredients together and stir into creamed mixture. Fold in nuts. Pour into a greased 8x8 baking pan. Bake 45 minutes at 350. Serve with caramel sauce poured over top.

Caramel Sauce: Stir 1/4 cup butter, 1/3 cup brown sugar, and 1/4 cup cream or canned milk over medium heat until it starts to thicken. Do not boil. Remove from heat. Stir in 1/2 tsp. vanilla.

Sweet Apple Crisp

3 medium apples	1/2 tsp. cinnamon
1/4 cup maple syrup	1/3 cup flour
3 Tbsp. butter	1/4 tsp. salt

Wash, core, and slice apples. Spread in small baking pan. Drizzle syrup over apples. Combine dry ingredients. Cut in butter until crumbly. Toss evenly over apples. Bake at 350 for 40-45 minutes. Serve with vanilla ice cream.

Applesauce Cookies

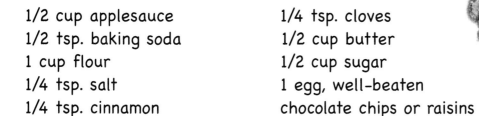

1/2 cup applesauce
1/2 tsp. baking soda
1 cup flour
1/4 tsp. salt
1/4 tsp. cinnamon

1/4 tsp. cloves
1/2 cup butter
1/2 cup sugar
1 egg, well-beaten
chocolate chips or raisins

Stir baking soda into applesauce and allow to sit while creaming butter, sugar, and egg together. Sift dry ingredients together. Mix applesauce with creamed mixture. Add dry ingredients and stir well. Fold in chocolate chips or raisins. Drop onto greased cookie sheet and bake at 400 for 10-12 minutes.

Spicy Apple Cookies

1 cup flour
1/2 tsp. baking soda
1/4 tsp. salt
3/4 tsp. cinnamon
1/4 tsp. nutmeg
1/4 tsp. ground cloves

3/4 cup grated apples
1/4 cup oil
1 egg
1/3 cup sugar
1/3 cup brown sugar
1/3 cup raisins

Sift dry ingredients together. Blend apples, oil, egg, and sugars together. Add dry ingredients and mix well. Add raisins (and nuts if desired). Drop onto a greased cookie sheet. Sprinkle cinnamon sugar on top. Bake at 350 for 12-15 minutes. Place on rack to cool.

Lemon Love Notes

Crust: 1 cup flour   1/4 cup powdered sugar
         1/2 cup butter   1/4 tsp. salt

Filling: 1 cup sugar   1/4 tsp. baking powder
         2 eggs   1/4 cup flour
         1/4 cup lemon juice   1/4 tsp. salt

Mix four crust ingredients together. Press into 8x8 baking pan. Bake at 350 for 15 minutes. Remove from oven. Meanwhile, combine remaining ingredients together. Spread lemon mixture over crust. Bake at 350 an additional 30 minutes. Sprinkle with powdered sugar.

Cherry Cheesecake Bars

1/4 cup flour   1/4 cup sugar
1/4 cup finely chopped walnuts   1 4-oz. package
1/4 cup flaked coconut   cream cheese
2 Tbsp. butter   1 egg
2/3 cup cherry pie filling   1/4 tsp. vanilla

Combine first four ingredients together. Press 2/3 of mixture into 8x8 baking pan. Beat sugar, cream cheese, egg, and vanilla together. Spread over crust and bake at 350 for 40 minutes. Remove from oven. Spread pie filling on cheesecake. Sprinkle with remaining crust mixture. Return to oven. Bake additional 20 minutes.

Never-Fail Sugar Cookies

1 1/2 cups flour
1/2 tsp. baking powder
1/4 tsp. salt
1/2 cup sugar

1/4 cup butter
1 egg
1/4 cup sour cream
1/2 tsp. vanilla

Sift dry ingredients together. Cream sugar and butter together. Stir in eggs, vanilla, and sour cream. Add flour mixture and stir well. Refrigerate until well chilled. Roll dough 1/4" thick. Cut shapes and place on greased cookie sheet. Bake at 350 for 10-12 minutes.

Snickerdoodles

3/4 cup flour
1/4 tsp. baking soda
1/4 tsp. salt
1/4 tsp. cream of tartar
1/4 cup butter
1/2 cup sugar
1 egg
1/4 tsp. vanilla

Take time to... say I Love You

Sift dry ingredients together. Cream sugar and butter together. Add eggs and vanilla and stir until well blended. Combine with flour mixture. Roll into balls. Make cinnamon sugar mix by combining 2 Tbsp. sugar and 1 tsp. cinnamon. Roll balls in cinnamon sugar and place on ungreased cookie sheet. Bake at 375 for 10-12 minutes.

No-Bake Cookies

3 Tbsp. butter
2/3 cup sugar
1 Tbsp. cocoa
1/4 tsp. salt

3 Tbsp. milk
1/4 cup peanut butter
1/2 tsp. vanilla
1 1/4 cups quick oats

Melt butter in saucepan. Remove from heat and stir in cocoa, sugar, and salt until well blended. Stir in milk. Bring to a boil. Remove from heat and stir in peanut butter, vanilla, and quick oats. Drop onto waxed paper or buttered cookie sheet.

Texas Sheet Cake

1/2 cup flour
1/2 cup sugar
1/4 cup butter

1 Tbsp. cocoa
1/4 cup water
2 Tbsp. buttermilk

1/4 tsp. baking soda
1 egg
1/8 tsp. salt

Mix flour and sugar. Melt butter in saucepan. Stir in cocoa until well blended. Add water and bring to a boil. Pour over flour mixture and stir. Add remaining ingredients and mix well. Pour into a greased 8x8 baking pan. Bake at 400 for 20 minutes. Spread icing while cake is still hot.

Icing: Melt 2 Tbsp. butter in saucepan. Remove from heat. Stir in 1 tsp. cocoa, 1/2 tsp. vanilla, and 2 Tbsp. milk. Add 2/3 cup powdered sugar and beat until smooth. Stir in 1/4 cup chopped walnuts if desired.

Chocolate Sandwich Cookies

1/2 box devil's food cake   1 egg   6 Tbsp. butter

Combine ingredients. Drop spoonfuls onto greased cookie sheet. Bake at 350 for 10 minutes. They will not look done but remove from oven and let cool. Ice bottom of one cookie generously with creamy filling. Place bottom side of another cookie on frosting like a sandwich.

Creamy filling: Soften 1 Tbsp. butter and 2 oz. cream cheese. Cream together with 2/3 cup powdered sugar.

Chocolate Zucchini Cake

1/3 cup vegetable oil	1 cup flour
2/3 cup zucchini	2/3 cup sugar
1 egg	1/2 tsp. baking soda
1 tsp. vanilla	3 Tbsp. cocoa
1/4 cup milk	1/4 tsp. salt

Pour 1/3 cup oil in blender. Chop small pieces of zucchini and drop in oil. Blend a few pieces at a time until mix reaches the 1-cup mark. Add egg, vanilla, and milk and blend completely. Sift dry ingredients together. Pour zucchini mixture into dry ingredients and stir well. Pour into greased 8x8 baking pan. Bake at 350 for 30-40 minutes. Cool and frost with chocolate icing.

Chocolate Icing: Beat 3 Tbsp. milk, 2 Tbsp. butter, 1 tsp. cocoa, and 1 cup powdered sugar until creamy.

☆Oatmeal Raisin Cookies

1 cup flour	1/3 cup sugar
1/4 tsp. baking powder	1/2 cup butter
1/4 tsp. baking soda	1 egg
1/4 tsp. salt	1 tsp. vanilla
1/2 tsp. cinnamon	1/2 cup raisins
1/2 cup brown sugar	1 cup quick oats

Sift dry ingredients together. Cream sugars, butter, egg, and vanilla together. Blend dry mixture with creamed mixture. Add raisins and oats and stir well. Drop onto ungreased cookie sheet and bake at 375 for 10-12 minutes. Place on rack to cool.

Pumpkin Chocolate Chip Cookies

1 1/2 cups flour	1/4 tsp. ginger	1/2 cup pumpkin
1 tsp. baking powder	1/4 tsp. ground cloves	2 eggs, well-beaten
1/2 tsp. baking soda	1/2 cup sugar	1/2 cup chocolate chips
1/4 tsp. salt	1/4 cup brown sugar	
1/2 tsp. cinnamon	1/3 cup oil	

Sift dry ingredients together. Blend pumpkin, sugars, oil, and eggs together. Stir dry ingredients into pumpkin mix. Add chocolate chips and stir well. Drop onto greased cookie sheet. Bake at 375 for 12-15 minutes.

The Best Brownies Ever

1/2 cup butter
4 Tbsp. cocoa
1 cup flour
1/2 tsp. baking powder

1/4 tsp. salt
2 eggs
1 cup sugar
1 tsp. vanilla

Melt butter in saucepan. Remove from heat and stir in cocoa until well blended. Add eggs and stir until blended. Do not over-stir, or batter will rise too high and then fall. Sift dry ingredients together and stir into cocoa mix. Spray or grease an 8x8 baking pan. Spread batter evenly in pan. Bake at 350 for 20 minutes. Brownies should still be gooey when they first come out of the oven.

Chocolate Chip Cookies

1 1/2 cups flour
1/2 tsp. baking powder
1/2 tsp. baking soda
1/4 tsp. salt
1/2 cup butter

1/3 cup brown sugar
1/2 cup sugar
1 egg, well-beaten
1 tsp. vanilla
1/2 cup chocolate chips

Sift dry ingredients together. Cream butter and sugars together. Add eggs and vanilla and stir well. Stir the dry ingredients into the creamed mixture. Fold in chocolate chips. Drop onto ungreased cookie sheet. Bake at 375 for 10-12 minutes. Remove immediately from pan and cool on rack.

Peanut Butter Cookies

3/4 cup flour
1/2 tsp. baking soda
1/4 tsp. salt
1/4 cup butter
1/4 cup peanut butter

1/4 cup brown sugar
1/4 cup sugar
1 egg
1/4 tsp. vanilla

Sift dry ingredients together. Cream butter, peanut butter, and sugar. Add egg and vanilla and stir well. Add dry ingredients and stir until blended. Roll dough into 2" balls. Dip in sugar and place sugar-side-up on ungreased cookie sheet. Press fork tines into top of cookie to make a grid pattern. Bake at 375 for 10-12 minutes. Place on rack to cool.

Peanut Butter Bars

Follow above recipe, but decrease flour to 1/4 cup and add 1 cup rolled oats. Spread cookie dough in 8x8 cake pan. Bake at 375 for 10-12 minutes. Remove from oven and spread 1/3 cup peanut butter over cookie while still hot. Make chocolate frosting and spread over cookie. Cut into bars.

Chocolate Frosting:
2 Tbsp. butter
2 Tbsp. milk

1 1/2 cups powdered sugar
2 Tbsp. cocoa

Beat ingredients together until creamy. Add more powdered sugar if needed.

Chewy Caramel Popcorn

2/3 cup brown sugar
1/3 cup butter
1/4 cup corn syrup

1/2 tsp. salt
1/2 tsp. vanilla
2 quarts popped corn

Pop enough corn to make 2 quarts. Remove unpopped kernels. Butter a large bowl. Put popcorn in bowl. In a saucepan, melt butter and add brown sugar, corn syrup, and salt. Bring to a boil, stirring constantly. Simmer 3 minutes. Do not stir. Remove from heat and stir in vanilla. Pour caramel syrup over top. Mix well with a wooden spoon.

Invest in a hot-air popper. They make popping easy and it's less calories.

Paper-Bag Popcorn: Pop 1 cup popcorn in a hot-air popper. Melt 1/4 cup butter. Stir in 1/2 tsp. salt. Pour over popcorn and stir well. Dump popcorn into a clean paper bag and shake fast and hard. Eat popcorn right out of the bag.

Cheesy Popcorn

2 quarts popped corn
3 Tbsp. butter

1 cheese packet from a box
  of macaroni and cheese

Melt butter. Pour melted butter over popcorn and dump into a clean paper bag. Shake popcorn quickly. Sprinkle powdered cheese over popcorn and shake bag one more minute.

Grandma's Chewy Caramels

1/2 cup sugar	1/2 cup corn syrup
2 Tbsp. butter	1/2 cup canned milk

Combine sugar and corn syrup in a heavy pan. Cook and stir over medium heat. Bring to a boil, stirring constantly until thick. Turn heat to high and add butter. Stir until melted. Add milk in a slow, steady stream, stirring constantly. Cook to a firm ball stage. (Drop a tiny amount of candy in a cup of cold water. When the candy forms a firm ball, it is ready.) Remove from heat. Pour onto buttered cookie sheet. When cool, cut into squares and wrap in waxed paper.

Fruity Popcorn

1/4 cup Jello mix (any flavor)	2 Tbsp. water
1/3 cup butter	2 quarts popped corn

Pop enough corn to make 2 quarts. Remove unpopped kernels. Butter a large bowl. Put popcorn in bowl. Melt butter in a saucepan. Add water and Jello. Stir until Jello is completely dissolved. Bring to a boil, stirring constantly. Remove from heat. Pour syrup over popcorn. Mix well with a wooden spoon.

Fruity Popcorn Balls

Follow directions for fruity popcorn. After syrup has been mixed into popcorn, butter your hands. Press handfuls of popcorn together to form balls. Wrap with plastic wrap.

Honey-Nut Snack Mix

2 cups corn squares cereal
2 cups graham squares cereal
1/2 cup nuts (any kind)
1/2 cup coconut

1/4 cup raisins
2 Tbsp. butter
2 Tbsp. sugar
2 Tbsp. honey

Mix cereals, nuts, coconut, and raisins together. Melt butter in a heavy saucepan. Add remaining ingredients. Cook and stir over medium heat. Bring to a boil. Boil for 3 minutes. Pour hot syrup over cereal mix. Stir well with a wooden spoon.

Yogurt Pretzel Mix

6 oz. white chocolate chips
2 Tbsp. vanilla yogurt

2 cups pretzel mix
1/2 cup raisins

You can use any variety of pretzel mix for this recipe. Combine pretzel mix and raisins in a bowl. Melt white chocolate chips. Stir in vanilla yogurt. Pour over mix. The yogurt won't cover all pieces completely, but it tastes great this way.

Party Snack Mix

2 Tbsp. butter
2 tsp. ranch dip mix
1/4 tsp. salt

1 cup cheese crackers
1/2 cup bagel chips
1 cup pretzels

1/2 cup rye chips
2 cups corn
    squares cereal

Melt butter. Add salt and dip mix. Stir well. Mix remaining ingredients in a large bowl. Pour butter over mix. Bake at 250 for 30 minutes, stirring often.

Green Onion Cheeseball

1 4-oz. package cream cheese
1/4 cup chopped green onions

1 tsp. Worcestershire sauce
1/3 cup smashed walnuts

Beat cream cheese until soft. Stir in Worcestershire sauce and green onions. Form into a ball. Smash walnuts by placing them in a sturdy zip-top bag and pressing a rolling pin over them until nuts are crumbly. Pour nuts onto a plate. Roll cheeseball in nuts until covered. Serve with crackers.

Ham Roll-ups

3-4 sandwich ham slices
1 4-oz. package cream cheese

2 green onions (cut the
  length of the ham slice)

Soften cream cheese and spread a thin amount over entire ham slice. Place green onion at one end of ham slice and roll tightly. Cut ham rolls into 2" pieces. Serve with crackers.

Cheese-Stuffed Celery

3-4 ribs celery (cut in 3 pieces)
cheese spread
1 4-oz. package cream cheese

1/4 cup crushed pineapple
1/4 tsp. salt
1 tsp. apple cider vinegar

Stuff cheese spread down centers of 1/2 of the celery pieces. Mix remaining ingredients together. Stuff remaining celery pieces with pineapple mixture.

My Favorite Recipes

My Favorite Recipes

My Favorite Recipes

_____

_____

_____

_____

_____

_____

_____

_____

_____

_____

_____

_____

_____

_____

_____

_____

_____

_____

_____

_____

No Success can compensate for FAILURE in the HOME David O. McKay

My Favorite Recipes

_____
_____
_____
_____
_____
_____
_____
_____
_____
_____
_____
_____
_____
_____
_____
_____
_____
_____
_____
_____
_____
_____
_____
_____
_____